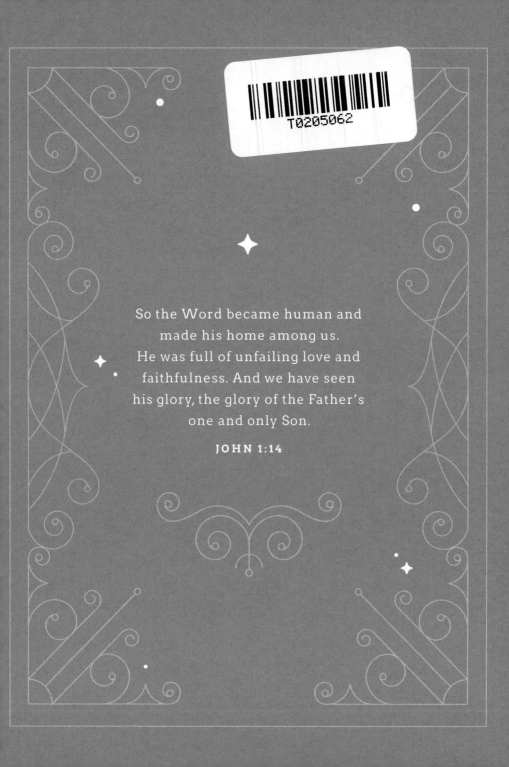

So the Word became human and
made his home among us.
He was full of unfailing love and
faithfulness. And we have seen
his glory, the glory of the Father's
one and only Son.

**JOHN 1:14**

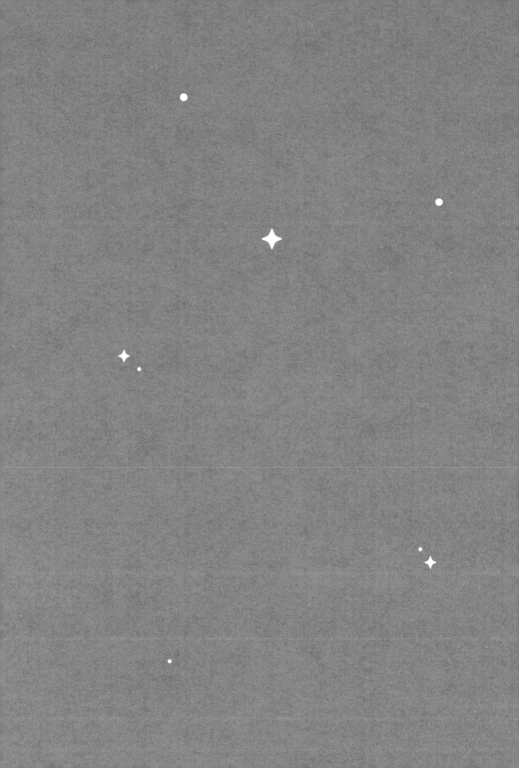

# MERRY AND BRIGHT

Rediscover the Hope, Peace, and Joy of Advent

# MERRY & BRIGHT

JULIE FISK • KENDRA ROEHL • KRISTIN DEMERY

TYNDALE
MOMENTUM®

*A Tyndale nonfiction imprint*

Visit Tyndale online at tyndale.com.

Visit Tyndale Momentum online at tyndalemomentum.com.

*Tyndale*, Tyndale's quill logo, *Tyndale Momentum*, and the Tyndale Momentum logo are registered trademarks of Tyndale House Ministries. Tyndale Momentum is a nonfiction imprint of Tyndale House Publishers, Carol Stream, Illinois.

*Merry and Bright: Rediscover the Hope, Peace, and Joy of Advent*

Designed by Eva M. Winters

Edited by Donna L. Berg

Published in association with the literary agency of Books & Such Literary Management, www.booksandsuch.com.

For information about special discounts for bulk purchases, please contact Tyndale House Publishers at csresponse@tyndale.com, or call 1-855-277-9400.

ISBN 978-1-4964-8748-3

Printed in China

| 30 | 29 | 28 | 27 | 26 | 25 | 24 |
|----|----|----|----|----|----|----|
| 7  | 6  | 5  | 4  | 3  | 2  | 1  |

*Thank you to all the women who have cheered us on—*
*including our agent Cynthia, Kara and the Tyndale team,*
*Melissa from Barnes & Noble, Lindsay and the White Peony crew—*
*as well as all those who have mentored, encouraged, believed in,*
*and prayed for us along the way. We're grateful for you.*

# Introduction

AS KIDS, MY SISTER KRISTIN AND I (KENDRA) and our family would drive from Minnesota to North Dakota every year to spend several days over Christmas break with our grandparents. Since we only saw them once or twice a year, we always looked forward to the several-hour drive to be with them. Their little white house on Main Street was filled with so many things we loved: treats like fudge and lefse, Grandpa Hans's windup toys, hours of playing Yahtzee, and time spent singing Christmas carols accompanied by Grandma Jo on the piano.

One year, a massive snowstorm came through on the day we were supposed to leave our home. My parents were concerned. They were unsure when the roads would be clear enough to drive on safely but didn't want us to miss the holidays we had planned for so long.

We finally were able to pack up and leave a day or so later, making our way slowly through the freshly fallen snow. We pulled up in my grandparents' driveway many hours later than we'd hoped.

As a child, I remember feeling mildly disappointed to leave later than expected, but the anticipation of gifts, fun treats, Christmas lights, and games with family consumed my mind. My parents carried the stress of preparing food to bring with us, packing everything in the car, and hoping they hadn't forgotten anything. What was magical for me was stressful for them.

It's a simple example, but most of us can relate to the good feelings we attach to the Advent season being underlaid by moments of strife or stress. We long for a joyful Christmas but struggle to reconcile our idealized visions with our messy reality. As we prepare for Jesus' arrival, how can we embrace the season in a way that offers hope and good cheer rather than tension and stress? And how do we include others—in our neighborhood or community—who may need the same comfort that Advent promises?

The holidays have always been a source of stress for many of us, and that seems to be increasing. In fact, a recent poll from the American Psychiatric Association indicated that 31 percent of Americans expected to be more stressed over the holiday season than in the previous year—a 9 percent increase. We can face many significant stressors this time of year, from affording meals and gifts to traveling and worrying about having to talk politics. Those concerns are amplified by grief, family dynamics, and the hard-to-measure feeling that Christmas "should" be joyful—but often is not.[1]

Jesus wants us to show up on his doorstep, unvarnished and unafraid. He does not turn us away because of the messiness of our lives; instead, he encourages us to step into his light and experience his love. Through this Advent devotional, the three of us—Kristin, Julie, and Kendra—will uncover what it truly means to embrace the promise of Advent. As you read along with us, we'll discover together what the expectancy of Jesus' birth means. We'll be encouraged to find the hope, comfort, love, and joy that is available to each of us, and we'll see ways to extend that same hope to those around us.

Each day's reading will invite you to rediscover the season's joys by addressing internal struggles while shifting your focus outward to your family, your neighbors, and the larger community. We will gain hope and healing as we invite others in, find simple joys, and prepare room for Jesus in the landscape of our lives.

If, like us, you've struggled to reconcile all the stress with the fun and joy of the season, we offer an alternative—one in which we still take into consideration the difficult aspects, making adjustments where possible, but give to God what's beyond our control. As we do so, we will find that merry and bright is still within reach for each of us at Advent.

# Meeting Him in the Mess

*Because Joseph was a descendant of King David, he had to go to Bethlehem in*
*Judea, David's ancient home. He traveled there from the village of Nazareth in*
*Galilee. He took with him Mary, to whom he was engaged, who was now expecting*
*a child. And while they were there, the time came for her baby to be born.*

LUKE 2:4-6

I KNEW IT WAS INEVITABLE. As soon as I finished placing the
activities into our family calendar, I had all the proof I needed
that December would be busy. Nearly every day was filled with
appointments, notes, and to-dos that covered the calendar square
and wound along the edge of the page.

And although I knew the month included good and fun things,
I secretly dreaded it.

A week into December, I broke down after dinner.

"I'm already tired," I admitted to my husband as I wiped down
the counters. He paused and turned from washing dishes to look
at me.

"What do you mean, Kendra?" he asked.

"The month has only begun," I continued, "but already we have things scheduled almost every night, and it doesn't stop until Christmas. We're only a few days in, and I'm already behind on our Advent devotional reading with the kids. Our house is messy, I haven't finished decorating, and the thought of squeezing cookie baking and gift wrapping into the already full calendar stresses me out. In the grand scheme of things, it's not a big deal to feel a bit behind—there are far worse things—but it just feels like a lot."

"You want something to change," my husband said. It wasn't a question. I nodded, hopeful that he would have a solution. "Honestly? Me too."

"None of this is bad," I acknowledged, "but is this really what we want this season to be about? I want to do some fun things with the kids, but I don't want to lose Jesus in the middle of all of that. Is there a way to somehow find a good balance for our family?"

"I think so," he said, his voice thoughtful. "Let's make a plan."

That night, after putting our kids to bed, we pulled out our monthly calendar and began to reevaluate our schedule. We decided which events and obligations we wanted to keep and which we could let go of. And we planned how to incorporate the activities that were important to us and let go of the ones that weren't really necessary.

I went to bed feeling a little better. Although the weeks that followed weren't perfect—we still fell behind on our devotional readings, and our house was at times disorganized—I knew we were being intentional about focusing on the things that mattered during Advent. Anticipating Jesus' arrival, celebrating the season, and spending time with loved ones while also making room to be generous and invite others in—those were the activities we prioritized. Life was still untidy and imperfect, and I felt frazzled some days, but that was okay. God is still present even when our plans don't proceed as we envisioned. He is still moving. Still arriving. And he doesn't mind a little mess.

Our experience that year reminds me of the first Advent. The months leading up to the birth of Jesus were messy and unexpected, to say the least, as was the birth itself: the fact that he was born miles and miles from home—not even in a house, but in a stable. And that he was born among animals. Far from family. Placed in a manger filled with hay. Surrounded by shepherds who'd just come from the fields to see the baby born to be the Savior of the world. This scene was not what most of us would plan for or anticipate, yet that is what God chose to do, and none of it was unexpected to him.

If God was willing to come into the world in such a messy, unforeseen way, I don't believe he's put off by or disappointed in the messiness of our lives. In fact, maybe that's just the place he likes to show up the most. When we aren't perfectly coiffed but instead muddied by the cares of this world, when all we're holding is a glimmer of hope that the promise of Advent will bring something meaningful, wonderful, and joyful to our lives—that's his favorite time to meet us. In the mess.

Because of this truth, we don't have to hide or put on a show. We can be our whole selves, smooth and rough edges alike. He sees it all and loves us anyway. He is our peace, our comfort, even our joy.

As you prepare your heart and home this December, don't be afraid to get honest with God. Whether you are going into the Christmas season excited or trepidatious, he sees and knows your needs. Even now, he is near, and he desires nothing more than to meet you in the middle of your mess. The reality is that this balancing act will resurface every Christmas season. Life still moves quickly, and we must be intentional about making it what we want it to be. But we can trust that each year, as we continue to bring all of ourselves and our lives to Jesus, he will meet us once again.

*Lord, thank you that you don't expect perfection from us. You see our humanity and embrace us in our imperfections. As we begin the Advent season, may we wait expectantly for your arrival. May we look for all the big and small ways you meet us in the coming days—in our joy and happiness but also in our hard moments and busyness. May we remember to lean on your peace, comfort, and love this month and give ourselves the same grace that you extend to us. Amen.*

## Reflections:

1. Read Luke 2:1-20. Notice all the unexpected twists and messiness of Jesus' arrival. How does this comfort you as you consider your life circumstances?

2. Spend time being honest with God. Bring your stressors, fears, and joys to him. Ask him to help you let go of the cares that weigh you down, and open your heart to accept the peace he offers in this busy time of year.

3. How can you intentionally keep Jesus at the forefront of this Advent season? Consider areas in which you may need to make changes for this to happen.

## Embracing Advent:

*Look at your calendar for December and ask God to show you the activities you should keep and the ones you could let go of in the coming days. Decide for yourself, or have a conversation with your family so you are all in agreement.*

# Unconditionally Loved

*No power in the sky above or in the earth below—indeed,*
*nothing in all creation will ever be able to separate us from the*
*love of God that is revealed in Christ Jesus our Lord.*

ROMANS 8:39

I AM AN APPROVAL ADDICT in recovery (with frequent relapses). Too often, I find myself striving to earn the approval and love of people and, if I am honest, attempting to gain the approval and love of God.

My desire for approval impacts my life in curious, complicated ways, often leaving me sad, frustrated, regretful, and sometimes resentful.

During Advent, it looks like trying to be Julie, the Hostess with the Mostest, all the time and in every circumstance. I fret over everyone's feelings, even in situations beyond my control. I desperately want everyone to be filled with joy. I tend to count it as a personal failure when those around me experience disappointment, frustration, anger, or sadness, especially during the run-up to Christmas morning.

As an employee and volunteer, it looks like saying yes as a first instinct and then quietly struggling furiously to learn all the skills necessary to do that task I should not have said yes to. I learn new skills but learn them the hard way, often at the expense of time and energy that rightfully belong to people I love.

As a mom, it is the temptation to use my children as my report cards, tying my mothering identity directly to their successes and failures rather than understanding that great mothers can raise children who make terrible decisions and inadequate mothers can raise exceptional children. While I am called to be the best mother I can be, my children are individuals with free will, and I can neither take all the credit for their hard work and successes nor take all the responsibility for their mistakes.

As a wife, it is periodically forgetting that I am only 50 percent of the relationship and that both the good moments and the bad moments almost always belong, in part, to both my husband and me.

And, as a woman who loves and follows Jesus, I find myself trying to prove that I am worthy of his love, that my prayers are worth considering, and that I have somehow "earned" either the blessings or the hardships that come my way.

While attempting to live amicably and peaceably among others is a worthy goal, being addicted to the approval of others has unhealthy, warped repercussions when taken too far—for our own souls but also for those we love.

One of my favorite parts (I have several!) of the Advent story took place long before the actual birth of our Savior in a manger. We find it in Matthew 1:1-17, where Jesus Christ's human ancestry is recorded, going back forty-two generations to Abraham. (We see a similar recounting in Luke 3:23-38, tracing seventy-seven generations back to Adam and Eve.)

What is remarkable about Matthew's genealogy is the intentional inclusion of women, rather than the lineage running solely through the male ancestors as is done in Luke's version. In addition to the shock of naming women in the lineage in a patriarchal society, these women's backgrounds and histories *should have* precluded them from being in Jesus' lineage in the first place and should have prevented them from being singled out by Matthew in the second place! Let's take a closer look at two of these women, Rahab and Ruth.

We find the story of Rahab primarily in Joshua 2:1-24. Rahab, a Canaanite living in Jericho, was likely both an innkeeper and a prostitute. As an innkeeper, she met and hid two Israelite spies sent to scout the city before the Israelites attacked Jericho, and she ultimately assisted with their daring escape. As she helped them, she acknowledged the sovereignty of God and his favor upon his people. She pledged allegiance to him, asking that she and her family be spared during the subsequent invasion. Not only was God faithful to spare Rahab and her entire family, but it's revealed in Matthew's lineage of Jesus Christ that eventually, Rahab married Salmon (a direct ancestor of Jesus), and they had a son named Boaz (see Matthew 1:5).

Like Rahab, Ruth was a foreigner from an enemy people group, as we see in the Old Testament book named for her. As a Moabite, she would have worshiped other gods and had cultural traditions that were detested by God. Additionally, as a childless widow, she accompanied Naomi, her widowed mother-in-law, from the land of Moab back to Naomi's homeland of Israel. It is hard to imagine a status lower than the labels attached to Ruth: Moabite, widow, childless, poor. Yet we witness Ruth pledging her allegiance to both God and Naomi (see Ruth 1:16-18), and we see God's unconditional love for both women woven throughout their return to Israel and on through the courtship and eventual marriage of Ruth to Boaz. Yes, Rahab's son Boaz became Ruth's husband!

Of course, there are other specifically named "unworthy" ancestors in the lineage of Jesus, both male and female, including King David, who was an adulterer and murderer (see 2 Samuel 11). If that is not enough to convince you of God's unconditional love, consider that the church's early leaders also fell short of "earning" the love of God. Peter, a disciple of Jesus, denied knowing Jesus three times before the rooster crowed after Jesus' arrest in the garden of Gethsemane (see Matthew 26:69-75). Paul, the author of thirteen books in the New Testament, was once Saul, a fierce persecutor of the early church, until he encountered Jesus on the road to Damascus (see Acts 9:1-19).

These are but a few stories of unworthy men and women loved by God and called to serve him. Scripture is filled with unworthy, imperfect people, all loved by God, and all used by God to accomplish his will.

If Jesus' ancestry, as well as the individuals he commissioned to carry on his work after the Crucifixion, included such a motley crew of low-status, sinful individuals, is there not a place for you and me to embrace the unconditional love of God? And can we embrace that love this Advent season without striving?

My friend, the answer to that rhetorical question is an unequivocal, resounding *yes*! As we create Christmas magic for our loved ones, as we navigate disappointments due to sky-high expectations, as we make last-minute pivots for all the reasons that make December tricky, we can rest securely in the knowledge of God's unfathomable, unconditional, unsurpassable love, regardless of what we accomplish (or do not).

I invite you into an Advent filled to the brim with merry and bright, remembering that there is nothing that can separate you from the love of the one who holds you in the palm of his hand, who knows the number of hairs on your head, and who sent his one and only beloved Son as the most precious gift of all.

*Heavenly Father, thank you for the reminder that not only are we loved, but there is no distance we can travel, nothing we can do (or not do) to diminish your unconditional love for us. Gently nudge us when we are tempted into striving to earn your love rather than reveling in the understanding that your love is a gift freely given, unearned, and unearnable. Amen.*

## Reflections:

1. Read Romans 5:8. God loved us so much that he sent Jesus as the ultimate sacrificial gift while we were still sinners and before we chose to love God in return. In what ways can you pull this realization with you throughout our Advent journey?

2. In what ways have you been trying to earn the unconditional love of God? In what ways have you engaged in unhealthy approval addiction?

3. Every example in today's reading required a committing or recommitting of one's life to God. Write your own prayer of commitment or recommitment to God, following the examples of Rahab, Ruth, David, Peter, and Paul.

## Embracing Advent:

*Remind two family members or friends of God's unconditional love for them. Include today's verse and a note of encouragement in a message to them. Write yourself a similar note, and carry it with you or post it where you will see it regularly.*

# What's Most Important

*"Teacher, which is the most important commandment in the law of Moses?"*
*Jesus replied, "'You must love the LORD your God with all your heart, all*
*your soul, and all your mind.' This is the first and greatest commandment.*
*A second is equally important: 'Love your neighbor as yourself.'"*

MATTHEW 22:36-39

MY EYES SKIMMED THE LIST my oldest son had just handed to me.

"I might want to add a few more things," he said offhandedly as I flipped the paper over to see a complete second page of items for his Christmas list.

"I think you might have enough here, buddy," I said, not wanting to dampen his enthusiasm but not wanting to get his hopes up either.

"Yeah, but I just saw a commercial for one more thing . . ." His voice trailed off as he took the list from my hand and walked back toward his room. I sighed, wondering what to do. What he was asking for was not only unrealistic but also a bit selfish.

A few days later, Kristin, Julie, and I met for coffee. As I cupped the mug in front of me, grateful for its warmth, I shared the experience with them. They listened quietly, nodding understanding of my quandary.

"I want something more than this, you know?" I lamented. "Presents are fine, but that's not what I want Christmas to be about. I want to teach my kids to be more generous and not just focused on what they can get."

Kristin and Julie agreed. With young children of their own at home, they felt the same desire to push back against the consumerism that has overtaken the season.

"I have an idea, Kendra," my sister said. We leaned in as she began to tell us about the acts of kindness she'd been seeing on social media. "What if we did something like that? Together?"

For a moment, it sounded like a lot, but as she shared ideas—cookies for neighbors, thank-yous to teachers, holding the door for others, and shoveling the neighbor's driveway—our enthusiasm flared to life.

"They don't have to be big things or even cost money. We can pick some bigger things, but mostly, let's look for ways to do it in our everyday activities."

Julie and I nodded as our minds started simmering with the possibilities.

"Let's do it," Julie said, snagging a napkin from a nearby table and beginning to take notes.

It was a simple plan: one kind act each day. Our families would rotate, so we would each do one activity every three days. We'd post a picture on social media and describe what we'd done, which would keep us accountable and also encourage others to do the same. No act was too big or too small. We'd try to find things in our neighborhoods, community, country, and even the world.[1]

I left the coffee shop, encouraged to try something new. When I arrived home and explained to my husband what we were planning, he readily agreed that this was a good idea for our young family.

We told the kids our plan at dinner a few nights later. We gave examples and then told them they could each choose one of their own ideas that we could do together as a family. I printed off kindness lists found online so they could see the possibilities.

"But there's one other thing," I said as we finished, looking around the table as my kids' heads popped up. "This means we won't buy as many presents for ourselves because we want to use some of our finances for other people. You'll still get some presents—just fewer."

"Christmas is really about Jesus and showing our love for him by loving others," my husband added.

The kids nodded, albeit hesitantly.

"You'll see," I said, smiling. "This is going to be fun. I promise."

Over the next several weeks, it *was* fun. Our children began to scour the kindness lists, highlighting the options they would want to do, finding a passion for people and causes we hadn't ever discussed or even known about.

They decided to each pick out a toy for another child their age to be given at Christmas, and my oldest son found a program for homeless veterans that we bought supplies for and sent off together. We bought chickens and soccer balls for families overseas and brought diapers and supplies to a young mothers' program in our community. With each act, I would whisper to my kids, "This is what Christmas is about. This is one way we show our love for Jesus."

Although it wasn't always perfect—my kids still threw tantrums, complained about helping, and sometimes whined about what we were doing—they also felt the thrill of giving, of being a blessing to someone else. And that experience started our family on a trajectory of shifting the focus of Christmas back toward Christ.

Each year since that first one, our kids have known that we'll be coming up with a list of kindnesses to do for others, and they each have their favorites: making cookies to give to neighbors, buying gifts for kids in foster care, supporting veterans through Wounded Warrior programs, and more. We have all started to look around for the needs in our world and then to ask, "How can I help?"

Christmas has become a time to celebrate Jesus by noticing those in need and doing something, even a small thing, to alleviate or fill that need. But the beautiful thing is that this has developed in us a habit of noticing needs not just at Christmas but all year. My kids' sensitivity toward others doesn't end on December 25; they now notice needs and want to help any time a concern arises. And because we've already been doing kind acts, they feel empowered to meet needs any time of the year. That is one of the greatest (unanticipated) lessons we've all taken away from this addition to our Advent traditions.

Maybe you, too, have struggled to keep Christ at the forefront of Christmas. Many of us want to maintain some of the traditions we grew up with while also incorporating new ways to encourage an expectancy for Jesus and what that means for us. Doing kind acts is a practical way for us to show our kids what it means to love God and others in a tangible way they can understand—to see that Christmas isn't just about what we can get but what we can give. It's a lesson we can all learn at any age.

Pushing back against our culture's consumeristic, me-first mentality isn't easy. It won't be perfect—it doesn't have to be—but it is possible. It starts when we find ways to put Jesus' greatest commandment into practice each day. And in return, we find the joy and merriment this season is truly all about anyway.

*Lord, thank you for such a simple-to-understand commandment—loving God and loving others. Help us to live it out each day. May we look for ways to be generous and kind to those we come in contact with throughout our day. Inspire us to meet needs that come to us, both near and far. Give us a heart that notices needs and is moved with compassion to help those around us. And may we carry your love for others even beyond this season and into the new year. Thank you for your love and kindness to us. We love you. Amen.*

## Reflections:

1. Read Matthew 22:34-40. What surprises you about Jesus' answer to the Pharisees? What do you think they expected him to say?

2. What would it look like for you to love God and others well? What needs in your community or neighborhood could you help to meet in the coming weeks? Is there a cause you are passionate about that you could partner with to be a blessing during Advent?

3. What can you let go of in this current season to have more room to show kindness toward others? Carefully consider the plans already on your calendar to see if some could be eliminated.

## Embracing Advent:

*Make a plan for how you could start incorporating even just a few kind acts into your activities this Advent season.*

# Just for the Fun of It

*Always be full of joy in the Lord. I say it again—rejoice!*

PHILIPPIANS 4:4

"CAN YOU DROP THIS OFF FOR ME TOMORROW?" I asked my husband as we got ready for bed one night.

"Sure, Kristin," he said as he finished brushing his teeth and turned to look at me. "Which neighbor do you have this year?"

"I've got Joy," I said, mentioning a woman several houses down from ours.

He nodded in response. "I'll do it on my way to the gym in the morning."

*Can you drop this off for me* is a question I've asked my husband many times, especially in December. That's because nearly every year the ladies in our quiet cul-de-sac participate in a Secret Santa gift exchange.

Originally my neighbor Debbie's idea, it's still going strong after more than a decade.

After drawing a name, we spend Monday through Friday of the designated week secretly dropping off small daily gifts for that person—candy, nail polish, fuzzy socks, a small candle. Though I enjoy the exchange overall, I will say that I've never felt as conspicuously exposed as I do when trying to sneak a gift bag across the street on a Tuesday afternoon, hoping that no one is looking out their window or exiting their home.

There's nothing quite like slinking around the neighborhood as a grown adult, feeling like you're starring in a bad spy movie—thus, my reason for asking my husband to do the drop-offs in the early, predawn hours. In recent years, we've gotten smarter and outsourced gift delivery to the neighbor kids, who delight in dropping off brightly wrapped packages on porches when they arrive home from school in the afternoon.

On Saturday we cap the week by sharing brunch, exchanging a final gift, and revealing our identity.

Though I live next to these women all year, we rarely get to have in-depth conversations about life. Of course, we wave hello while watering plants, shoveling snow, or picking up packages at the mailbox, but this annual tradition helps ensure that we reconnect and catch up on everything that's happened over the last year. We've shed tears over lost loved ones, celebrated successes or job changes, and smiled over kids' antics. I look forward to brunch with my neighbors every year—just because it's fun.

All too often, holiday events are obligations. That's not to say we don't enjoy the work party, kids' orchestra concert, or umpteenth family gathering, but sometimes the feeling that our presence is required rather than requested can steal some of the joy.

How many things do we do at the holidays simply for the joy of it? Shouldn't we try to make room for fun?

In Ecclesiastes, the author makes it clear that we should counterbalance work with time spent enjoying food and the fruits of our labor, as these are gifts from God: "I recommend having fun, because there is nothing better for people in this world than to eat, drink, and enjoy life. That way they will experience some happiness along with all the hard work God gives them under the sun" (8:15). God gave us today, and he wants us to enjoy it like the gift it is—and even to rejoice in it.

Let's find reasons to celebrate that bring us joy and don't feel like obligations. We can—and should!—participate in annual activities like our neighborhood Secret Santa tradition with friends and neighbors. There's a certain joy in keeping something going every year, something that's just for the fun of it. Reconnecting with others brings joy to our lives and lightness to our spirit.

Though it can be challenging, I try to leave room in our calendar for fun, especially in December. For instance, my kids love doing a white elephant gift exchange. We go to a big-box store, give everyone a ten-dollar limit, and spend time choosing two gifts: one that we think is funny and one that is useful or delicious. (Unsurprisingly, everyone chooses candy as their second item.) At home, we wrap them and exchange them by playing a game.

We're also big on family movie nights (our long list of favorite Christmas movies and "fancy popcorn" with marshmallows and chocolate candies in it feature prominently); watching the stars from the warmth of our outdoor hot tub; and incorporating small acts of kindness for others, like leaving "candy bombs" full of treats and a thoughtful card on cars in the parking lot at our local hospital. Those annual traditions aren't necessary but are always meaningful, and we look forward to them every year.

Increased candy intake aside, those moments of fun can help me get off the merry-go-round of busyness and fully enjoy the gift of the season rather than constantly fueling the rush from one event or task to the next.

If a neighborhood brunch feels too burdensome, start small. There's no need to add more to our calendar, feel overwhelmed, or think we must force the fun. Instead, consider something you're already doing, like eating meals three times a day. Could you share your morning cup of coffee with a neighbor? Have lunch with a coworker or grab a smoothie with someone after a workout at the gym?

Or maybe there are other activities you could overlap with a friendly visit. Could you plan to grocery shop at the same time as a friend so you can visit together while strolling through the aisles? Stay after church for a few extra minutes to chat with someone? Call a friend while you wait for a child to finish basketball practice? Text someone on your lunch break? Or, if you're feeling overloaded, consider that rest can be an underrated form of fun—and take a break or sneak in a catnap.

Holiday celebrations and traditions aren't just something we do with family or because they're mandatory but because life is meant to be enjoyed. Today, let's choose to have fun.

*Dear Jesus, thank you for the gift of fun. Life is precious, and it's meant to be enjoyed. Instead of hurrying through our days or running from one task to the next, remind us to stop and find something to do just because it's enjoyable. Help us to remember that even routine things, like daily meals, can be opportunities to add a little joy to our lives. May we always remember to thank you for the things in this world that are fun and spark delight. Amen.*

## Reflections:

1. Read 1 Corinthians 10:31. What do you think it means to do everything for the glory of God? What does that look like in your life? Does it change at all during the holiday season? Why or why not?

2. How many events and activities do you do at this time of year simply because they are obligations? How could you make time to include more things just for fun?

3. Are there fun traditions, events, or activities you have done in previous years that you could incorporate again this year? Or are there new activities you have always wanted to try with your family? What might that look like?

## Embracing Advent:

*Choose an activity or event you want to do simply for fun, then find a time to do it in the next few weeks.*

# Faithful Response to a Faithful God

*Mary responded, "I am the Lord's servant.*
*May everything you have said about me come true."*

LUKE 1:38

I DON'T KNOW WHY, but for many years, I (Kendra) had the impression that Mary was meek, mild, observant, and religious. Like the rule-following kids who always obeyed instructions, listened to the teachers, and never got into trouble.

Maybe it was because she questioned very little of the angel's news other than to ask how it could be, practically speaking, because she was a virgin. Beyond that, we're simply told that she responded, "May everything you have said about me come true."

But as I've read more deeply into the story, especially the implications of being a pregnant woman, betrothed but not married,

I've realized what a massive leap of faith she took in saying yes. She had no idea how her family or Joseph would respond. Would they shun her? What would her community think? And how would she tell them?

We're told that an angel came to Joseph, encouraging him to remain engaged to Mary. Otherwise, he had planned to divorce her, albeit quietly (see Matthew 1:19-25). But Mary didn't know that when she said yes to God. And she would have risked being shunned and abandoned by Joseph at best and, at worst, being stoned to death if he'd accused her of adultery.

This was no small ask and no small yes. Mary took significant risks to follow God's direction. She said yes when many others would probably have said no. She said yes to a decision that would change her life. Her family's life. Her reputation. Her future. Everything.

But instead of responding in fear or dread, she responded in faith. When her cousin Elizabeth told her she was blessed among women, she replied,

Oh, how my soul praises the Lord.
    How my spirit rejoices in God my Savior!
For he took notice of his lowly servant girl,
    and from now on all generations will call me blessed.
For the Mighty One is holy,
    and he has done great things for me.

He shows mercy from generation to generation
　　to all who fear him. . . .
He has helped his servant Israel
　　and remembered to be merciful.
For he made this promise to our ancestors,
　　to Abraham and his children forever.

LUKE 1:46-50, 54-55

Mary praised God and had the foresight to understand the promises he made long ago to Abraham and his children—Abraham, the one who'd been promised offspring as numerous as the stars in the sky before he'd ever fathered a child (see Genesis 15). She was now seeing the promise made to Abraham coming to fruition in the approaching birth of this child, Jesus.

Abraham's descendants certainly are as unnumbered as the stars in the sky, since Jesus, the Son of Man and Son of God, invites each of us into the family of God. No one is left out. Everyone is welcome, Jew and Gentile alike. There are no longer those who are in and those who are out. Jesus casts a wide net, inviting the most shunned of society into his circle of friends, even calling them family.

And Mary would have witnessed all of this. She must have had moments of extreme pride and pain as she watched Jesus begin his ministry, face criticism, be killed, and then be raised from the dead. It could not have been an easy road.

She birthed and nursed him and watched him grow as a child. She hugged him and rocked him to sleep, made sure he was fed and had a bed to sleep on. Like all good parents, she and Joseph would have ensured that his basic needs were met.

She saw him laugh and listened to him joke with his siblings. She observed as he learned how to be a carpenter, working alongside Joseph. She was there when his public ministry began and witnessed his first miracle, turning water into wine. She saw the crowds of people who followed him, watching them love him . . . and hate him. She witnessed or heard about him healing and inviting in those who had been cast out by society. She listened to his teachings.

Mary would have known when Jesus entered Jerusalem with worshipers laying palm branches at his feet, only to be arrested and beaten just a few days later. She was there when he was crucified and laid in a grave and then would have heard of his resurrection and ascension. She was a witness to his life, beginning to end.

And all along, Mary remained faithful. In return, God was faithful to her. Jesus made sure she was taken care of upon his death (see John 19:26-27). We should remember her not as superhuman but as someone who believed that God's will and purpose for her life were better than anything she could plan out on her own. She was a light for others to see. And it all came from a simple yes to God's request years earlier.

Mary's story challenges me. Being a rule follower myself, I wonder how easily I would say yes if put in her situation. I'm not someone who would want to risk having others talk negatively about me, being shunned by my community, or—even worse—being killed for a decision I've made. It could not have been easy.

And yet I sincerely want to pursue God with everything inside me, knowing that saying yes sometimes comes at a cost—to reputation, relationships, financial stability. All areas of our lives can certainly be affected.

It's not always uncomplicated to follow God's lead. Just like Mary, we may find immense purpose in being obedient to him, but we may still experience pain or even heartbreak. Did she know when she said yes to God that she would also be there one day to watch her son suffer and die? I don't know. But do I think she would change any of it? I'm sure she would not.

You and I are not so different from Mary. If we are sensitive to God and the Holy Spirit, we, too, may find ourselves faced with a decision that could change the course of our lives. But if we're willing to take a leap of faith, trusting that God is good even in the hard times, we will say, as Mary did, "I am the Lord's servant."

When we follow God's plan for our lives, and when we get to the end of it all, we'll look back and not regret obeying him and saying yes. No matter the cost.

*Lord, thank you for Mary and the example she set that we can learn from today. Help us to be willing to say yes to you in anything you call us to do. Give us courage as we remember that you will be with us, always, in good and challenging times. May we have the boldness to pursue you in big and small ways, and help us to be a light to the people around us. Thank you for your faithfulness to us, and help us to remain faithful to you and all that you call us to do every day. Amen.*

## Reflections:

1. Read Luke 1:26-38. Imagine being in Mary's position. How do you think you would respond? How would you respond if you were in Joseph's position?

2. What character qualities do you find in Mary? Do you see any of them in yourself? How could you strengthen and develop these traits?

3. Think about a time in your life when you said yes to God, despite the challenges involved. What was the outcome? What did you learn that could be applied to your current challenges?

4. How has God asked you to step out in faith lately? Have you said yes? If not, what is holding you back? How could you follow Mary's example and be able to say yes?

## Embracing Advent:

*Determine to say yes to what God is asking of you today.*

# Reclaiming Peace

*I am leaving you with a gift—peace of mind and heart.*
*And the peace I give is a gift the world cannot give.*
*So don't be troubled or afraid.*

JOHN 14:27

THAT CAN'T BE RIGHT.

With a furrowed brow, I (Julie) reread the coach's letter to parents, laser focused on the paragraph laying out not one, not two, but *four* competitions scheduled in December, two of which were on school nights.

Four major events, including an expectation to volunteer. Sighing as I added those dates to my family's calendar, I eyed the obligations already scheduled in overlapping formation on those precious weekends during Advent. Angsty anxiety rears its ugly head when my December calendar starts filling with events over which I have little control.

It wasn't twenty-four hours later that my friend confessed her own loss of Advent peace. Her teens were the oldest grandkids in the extended family, and she was fretting about how the aunts (her sisters) would engage with them during an extended Christmas visit. The memory of a Memorial Day weekend debacle of misunderstandings and parenting style differences had her tied in proverbial knots.

Should she gently confront now, having conversations ahead of time to defuse possible tensions, and risk offending them? Or should she try to muddle through, keeping an illusion of peace for the sake of her aging parents? She longed for a visit filled with connection, joy, and laughter, but with so many personalities and opinions involved, she didn't know whether it was possible.

Someone else quietly admitted to job insecurity with their company in the midst of layoffs. With financial losses looming, the budget for Christmas morning, as well as for several expected gift exchange events, felt uncertain at best and teetered on impossible.

My widowed neighbor is navigating all of the "firsts" after losing her spouse. Christmas was her husband's favorite holiday, and she knows she cannot recreate the spectacle that has been a large part of their family's traditions.

A coworker's son is actively job hunting, and the rejection letters have been stressful and disheartening.

A church member is undergoing tests for a potentially difficult diagnosis.

There are so many different ways to lose our peace, aren't there? Too little time, rocky relationships, strained finances, grief, uncertainty about the future, medical diagnoses, hopes and expectations that do not match reality . . . The list is as infinite and varied as we are.

Is it possible to walk through December without losing our peace? I would argue that on our own, it's impossible. We have turned Christmas into a major production, complete with all the effort and expectations that get wrapped up in planning and executing such an event. I've yet to meet anyone who navigates those days between Thanksgiving and New Year's Day (what we in the US call the holiday season) with complete serenity: unruffled, unrattled, and unfazed.

But with God, it is not only possible, it is a promise. And today's verse reminds us that we can call upon that promise from moment to moment and day to day without shame. Every time our mind starts to veer toward that vortex of anxiousness over a situation, every time we're invited into worry by something we have read or heard, we have a choice.

We can *accept* that invitation into mental and physical chaos as we embrace all the what-ifs, should-haves, and if-onlys, allowing ourselves to get knotted up over regrets or consumed with what might happen. Dwelling on the past or always trying to predict and control the future robs us of the present moment and the joy and beauty to be found there. Or maybe the present moment is filled with the hardest hard. We might long to live in the past or future to escape the present discomfort.

But what if we *reject* the invitation into chaos, intentionally embracing the remarkable promise of today's verse: exchanging our worries for the peace that surpasses all understanding, Jesus' peace?*

I don't know about you, but my peace is fragile, thin, brittle, and easily fractured into a million tiny pieces. But the peace Jesus offers? His peace is unyielding, unmoving, unbending.

- It is a strong tower where we can seek shelter (see Proverbs 18:10).
- It is the firm foundation built upon rock that will not wash away in the floodwaters (see Matthew 7:24-27).
- It is the warmth of being tucked securely beneath his wings (see Psalm 91:4).
- It is the sheep recognizing the shepherd's voice, knowing he is safe to follow (see John 10:27-28).

That is the peace promised to us whenever we ask. When we accept the gift of Jesus' peace, the circumstances around us may not (immediately or otherwise) be changed, but our perspective shifts. We don't walk through obstacles or difficult seasons on our

---

* Please know, though, that sometimes God-given therapeutic interventions or medicines can play a key role. There is no shame or sin in seeking help even as we also pray.

own. We are known and seen by Jesus, our Savior and Redeemer (see Romans 10:9; Ephesians 1:7). And as our perspective shifts, hopefully our response shifts as well. We can quiet our mind and body before God, prayerfully asking what part requires an action (or inaction) from us, and what part belongs to God. As we move forward, continually choosing to stay in his peace, we can embrace the joy and beauty to be found in this Advent season no matter the circumstances.

*Heavenly Father, thank you that we can exchange our fragile peace for the peace Jesus unconditionally provides. Show us where we have been accepting invitations into chaos rather than intentionally clinging to your peace. Pull us back onto the firm foundation of our faith, keeping us grounded in the truth of your Word and your promises. Continually remind us that we are not alone, we are not forsaken or abandoned, and that we can return to your peace no matter how many times we have started to slip into confusion. Amen.*

## ℛeflections:

1. Read Philippians 4:6-7. Make a list of what steals your peace. Hand each item to God, asking him to guard your heart and mind. Each time you begin to worry, visualize handing it back to God, asking him to hold it.

2. If something from the past is stealing your peace, consider whether there needs to be repentance for your behavior (see 1 John 1:9) or forgiveness of someone else's behavior (see Colossians 3:12-13). Both need to be addressed with God first and then (sometimes) with others. Forgiving someone is between you and God, to free you from past hurts. It does not require that you allow damaging behavior to continue.

3. As you focus on staying in Jesus' peace, look for beauty, joy, and goodness in all their forms. Start by identifying one good thing for each of the five senses.

## ℰmbracing Advent:

*Who around you is feeling the tug toward anxiousness and worry? If you can, text them a prayer of peace that they can reread during challenging moments. Include Scriptures. Some favorites are John 14:27, John 16:33, and Philippians 4:6-7.*

# ℛeframing Our Expectations

*This is how Jesus the Messiah was born. His mother, Mary, was engaged*

*to be married to Joseph. But before the marriage took place, while she was*

*still a virgin, she became pregnant through the power of the Holy Spirit.*

*Joseph, to whom she was engaged, was a righteous man and did not want*

*to disgrace her publicly, so he decided to break the engagement quietly.*

MATTHEW 1:18-19

WE WERE WANDERING a department store at the mall when
something caught my eye. It was a beautiful cream-colored peacoat with big buttons, cut slim through the body. Fancy, but in
a timeless way. It looked like something Audrey Hepburn would
have worn in *Breakfast at Tiffany's*, or what you'd have seen on
Jackie Kennedy at a society event—1960s glamour wrapped up in
a 2000s coat. It was gorgeous but not the most sensible, especially
not in that cream color.

Ignoring my inner practicality, I pulled it off the rack and
looked around for a mirror.

"Hang on a sec. I want to try something on," I called out to my husband, who was still strolling ahead. He turned around and made his way back toward me just as I was shrugging it on.

"Did you find something you like, Kristin?" he asked.

It fit perfectly, even through the shoulders, which is rare for me. I couldn't help but admire the classic lines of it. But glancing at the price tag, I reluctantly placed it back on the hanger.

"Maybe another time," I sighed, common sense winning out.

By the time Christmas rolled around a couple of months later, I'd mostly forgotten about the coat. Yet when my husband slid a large box in front of me with a gleam in his eye, I wondered if he'd gotten it after all.

"Go ahead, open it," he urged, face alight with expectation.

It was beautifully wrapped in silver with a big bow on the front. As I slid my finger under the tape and removed the paper carefully, he practically vibrated with excitement.

Finally, I made it through the layers of paper, box, and tissue paper to reveal a cream-colored peacoat. It was beautiful, and it had buttons.

But it wasn't the one I'd loved.

"Oh—it's lovely," I managed to get out, but something in my voice must have given away my true reaction.

"What's wrong?" he asked. "Isn't that the one you liked?"

"Well . . . no," I said hesitantly, wanting to spare his feelings. He looked more upset than I felt. "But it's so pretty! Thank you so much!"

I could tell he was disappointed. He had been so sure it was the same one. I told him it was a beautiful coat, and though we could try to exchange it, I would still be happy either way.

It was a stroke of luck to find that the original coat was still there when we returned to the department store. The style that my husband had accidentally picked up was placed directly behind it on the rack. Years later, seeing that coat in my closet still makes me smile.

Though our Christmas morning gift exchange didn't go quite the way we'd expected, the truth is that things often go awry in life. Our expectations can foster or block our ability to feel true contentment with what we have.

It's one of the reasons I understand Joseph's situation in the Christmas story. After all, if any character in this account exemplifies what happens when reality doesn't match our expectations, it's Joseph. Granted, his experience involved much more serious life decisions than my coat mix-up, but it's often the little things that help us to see greater truths.

Scripture tells us that Joseph was a godly man. He and Mary were engaged to be married, meaning they had entered a formal betrothal. This only occurred after the groom submitted a contract (written or oral) to the bride's family. The couple was considered engaged once the bride's family agreed to the terms. The engagement lasted a year and wasn't easily dissolved.

In those days, Joseph's actions would have held a lot of power. So when he found out about Mary's pregnancy, his response could have had serious consequences. Understandably, Joseph would have wanted to consider his options carefully. After all, he was a righteous man in the Messianic line—descended from Abraham and David, among others—and would have been seeking a wife with the same level of righteousness.

Suppose he were to expose her to public shame. In that case, adultery had always been treated harshly in those times. In Judea, for example, the punishment for the woman was death by stoning—even when she was only betrothed and not yet married.[1]

Instead, Joseph chose the middle ground of breaking the engagement quietly, in which case a "writ of divorcement" was necessary. Since the writ would use vague language that didn't specify the reason for the broken engagement, Joseph could settle the matter without exposing Mary to further disgrace.[2]

Of course, everything changed when the angel visited Joseph, explained what was going on, and asked him to take Mary as his wife. By the time Jesus was born, Joseph was fully committed to his new family. I love how Matthew 1:25 notes the intentionality of Joseph's role: "And Joseph named him Jesus."

That doesn't mean that Joseph didn't continue to recalibrate his expectations. Instead of starting a life together with just him and Mary, they would immediately have a child. Not only that, but the whispers of doubt that clung to Mary and Joseph's reputations probably lingered long after Jesus was born. Joseph's expectation of pursuing a quiet life without others' judgment was likely long gone. But in its place, what an adventure Joseph must have experienced with Mary and Jesus! Raising the Son of God would have been a parenting endeavor unlike any other.

Though you and I have not faced Joseph's circumstances, we've likely experienced the burden of expectations, both our own and other people's. It's easy to have an idealized view of how family gatherings should occur, what topics of conversation can be covered, or even what kinds of gifts should be given. But people are messy, families can be broken, and the world's problems don't go away just because it's December.

Yet we can hope. Though we can't dictate our circumstances, we can reframe our expectations. Joseph needed discernment from God—who was not surprised by the circumstances he faced—and we do too. What does this look like, practically?

First, we can approach the Word of God, which has all the wisdom we need. Next, a few questions can help when we're trying to discern how to reframe a difficult situation: Is there another way to look at this? Is what I believe about it true? Is it helpful? And what "proof" do I have that the worst outcome will happen, anyway?

And lastly, we can pray over the situation, asking a few trusted friends if they'd do the same. As Christians, we are saved by the blood of the Lamb and the word of our testimony (see Revelation 12:11). Even the hard things—especially the hard things—are parts of our story.

Our expectations for good or ill can be fulfilled, but they just as often never come to pass. I've felt anxiety over situations that I assumed would go poorly but didn't, and I've been sidelined by hard conversations I didn't expect to have. But when I take the time to reframe my expectations through the lens of eternity—that this is all temporary, and that's okay—that mental space makes room for me to appreciate what I have.

Psalm 23:1 reads, "The Lord is my shepherd; I have all that I need." Though we may not—and likely will never—have all we *want*, we already have everything we need. In Jesus, we have a living hope that will not put us to shame. Though life will never be perfect, it can be good.

*Dear Jesus, thank you for helping us sift through the tangled topic of our expectations. This Christmas season can be full of unspoken expectations, dashed hopes, and missed opportunities. Give us your discernment as we seek to reframe our expectations through the lens of eternity. Give us long-range vision and the reminder that our temporary troubles are not more significant than the weight of your glory. Amen.*

# Reflections:

1. Have you ever felt like your expectations of what Christmas "should" be like don't match up with your reality? In those moments, what is your response?

2. What can we learn from Joseph and the role he played in the Christmas story? How might his response influence our own when life turns out differently than we'd anticipated?

3. Read 2 Corinthians 10:5 and Philippians 4:7. How can taking every thought captive and taking our worries to Jesus in prayer help us reframe our expectations?

# Embracing Advent:

*Practice reframing your expectations this week. When something doesn't go the way you'd expected it to, ask these questions: Is there another way to look at this situation? Is what I believe about it true? Is it helpful? Remember that even if you can't find the bright side, you can still find meaning in what's going wrong.*

# Embracing Advent Hospitality

*Don't forget to show hospitality to strangers, for some who have
done this have entertained angels without realizing it!*

HEBREWS 13:2

"HEY, JULIE! What about this tree? It's purple!"

A glance at my friend Ling had me grinning. She, her son, and
my kids were hugging a precut tree spray-painted an awful shade of
bright Vikings purple with cheesy expressions on their faces. As I
drew near, I noticed a certain wistfulness in my third-grade daughter's eyes.

"Hmmm. These are kinda little," I responded, "and I think we
wanted a big one to fit all our ornaments. Shall we see what we can
find down that row of big, fluffy trees?"

Winking at my daughter, I linked arms with her and whispered,
"Let's show our friends how we cut down a tree with Daddy's saw

instead of settling for one of these already chopped-down ones. Does that sound good?" And with that, the kids dashed pell-mell into the forest of available trees, with Ling, Aaron (my husband), and me hurrying to catch up.

My children have been enrolled in a Mandarin immersion program at our local public school since kindergarten, and that means we've had the opportunity to invite visiting Chinese teachers and interns into our family adventures for over a decade. During the three years Ling taught in our program, she and her young son became frequent visitors in our home and on our family outings. We ate meals together, trading off cooking American and Chinese styles. They joined us for major holidays, a road trip to Mount Rushmore, and whatever fun local events we thought might spark an interesting cultural exchange.

We discovered that our traditions and adventures became all the more memorable and enjoyable when Ling and Chang joined us. So when they returned to China, we temporarily adopted the next batch of visiting teachers and interns each subsequent year.

But here's the thing: hospitality doesn't require knowing people from the far corners of the earth, planning elaborate excursions, or even having magazine-worthy spaces for entertaining. Our first house was a two-bedroom rambler circa 1960 with its original seafoam green siding and the "vintage" yellow countertops covered in geometric orange triangles. Trust me when I say we owned that home during the awkward period when those eclectic design choices were just plain outdated rather than retro-cool.

We threw some of the biggest parties of our marriage in that small space, inviting the entire young adult group from church over for game nights and Christmas parties. I laugh to think of the fire codes we may have bent and the fun we had crammed into a tiny living room and kitchen before spilling out into our unremarkable urban backyard.

People return to our current house each Halloween because we've become known for our roaring driveway bonfire with a hot cocoa bar, s'mores, and—*gasp*—full-size candy bars, not because we love Halloween (at best, I barely tolerate it), but because we've discovered that it's easier to connect with our neighborhood and surrounding neighborhoods on that particular night than any other night of the year, and we will seize that opportunity.

In a world that is increasingly connected online and yet ever lonelier in person, we've been surprised over and over with how deeply impactful an invitation to a gathering or activity, even the simplest ones, has proven to be. And, for people who love Jesus, hospitality is essential, both to others who share our faith (see Romans 12:13; Galatians 6:10) and in the broader community (see Hebrews 13:2; 1 Peter 4:9).

So, what does hospitality look like during Advent when we are already pulled in a million different directions? Here are some practical considerations as you contemplate hospitality done your way during this already-busy season.

1. Who might you invite to already-planned activities or events without creating additional work? For several years in a row, our host's neighbors joined us for Thanksgiving dinner. They were a young family far from home, and pulling four extra chairs around the Thanksgiving table was literally the only extra work required from any of us. Their children fit right in with our pack of cousins, and we had really funny, interesting conversations about the differences between Minnesota and their home state of Texas.

2. Is there an older coworker, church member, or neighbor who might be missing the (mostly) joyous Advent atmosphere created by young children? For a time, our next-door neighbors were an older couple whose grandchildren lived several hours away. We didn't understand how much they missed the chaos of dinner with toddlers until they joined our rowdy patio dinner one evening. As Mark hugged me goodbye, his eyes teared up, and he told me how delightful it'd been to be around our family and how much they missed their grandkids. As a young mom, I simply had no idea my raucous crew could be a gift. Who might love to join your young family for a car ride to look at Christmas lights or for a chance to build a snowman in the backyard?

3. Do you live near a university? Often, a department or office is tasked with helping international students join a local family for holiday meals or other outings as a cultural exchange. If your family cuts down a tree at a tree farm, this is a fun cultural event for international students that adds nothing to your plans besides coordinating a ride. Other ideas include a cookie exchange, walking through an outdoor holiday market, sledding, snow tubing, or your Christmas Eve or Christmas Day meal. The gift of inclusion in a new cultural adventure will be a memory that lasts a lifetime—for both of you!

4. What about hosting a potluck evening with an ugly sweater contest or a Farkle tournament for your church community, coworkers, neighbors, fellow soccer parents—the list is as varied as our unique lives. It's an easy way to throw a party without the pressure of cooking for everyone. We've learned to let people spill into the backyard if the weather is decent; otherwise, we fill the house with folding chairs and let folks chat and eat without worrying about setting up card tables.

5. Consider your unique circumstances and stage in life as you figure out what works best right now. The types of hospitality that worked for me with toddlers don't always work for me with busy teenagers, and vice versa. And that's okay. Whether we have toddlers or teenagers, whether we are married or not, whether we are retired or working full-time—these all impact

what hospitality looks like for us this particular Advent. We can be hospitable, even as we honor where we are.

I've never regretted inviting people into my family's activities and events, and I've almost always found myself unexpectedly blessed in the process. And what is the point of a merry and bright Advent if we aren't inviting others into our joyous celebrations as we acknowledge our Savior's birth?

*Heavenly Father, show us how we can be inviters this Advent season without adding more work or stress to our already-full plates. Help us brave the risk of obedience in extending invitations, allowing you to be sovereign over whether that invitation is accepted. May we see those around us with your eyes, attuned to those who might be lonely or grieving this Advent season. And, as we practice hospitality, make the burden light, especially during this time of year. Amen.*

## Reflections:

1. Think about fears you have around hosting or hospitality. What's the worst thing that might happen? Now read Galatians 5:13. What God-honoring good might come from your hospitality? How could you minimize your fears while maximizing the good?

2. Think of a time when someone invited you to an activity, especially during a season of loneliness. How did it make you feel? Ask someone else to share a similar experience. What resulted from that invitation?

3. Think of two people who have been an example of excellent hospitality. Ask them to share their best tips for hosting. Have you experienced a time when hospitality was not handled well? What did you learn?

## Embracing Advent:

*Pick one activity or event in which you can easily include a hospitality component. Commit to extending that invitation before you crawl into bed tonight.*

# Heavenly Bruschetta

*Aaron and I have spent the last decade tweaking this recipe we found in an old magazine. We use it for hosting, holiday meal pre-snacking, and at-home date nights. If you come to my house more than three times, you'll be served our version of bruschetta. It is vegetarian and can easily be made vegan. The bruschetta topping can also be made ahead and refrigerated or frozen. But the thing I love most is that it is easy-peasy-lemon-squeezy to make and yet tastes like I labored for hours.*

## INGREDIENTS

- 2  14.5-ounce cans diced tomatoes with basil, garlic, and oregano (we use Del Monte; can also substitute 2 cups, chopped, of any flavorful fresh tomato for one can)
- ½  cup sun-dried tomatoes packed in oil, chopped
- 3  cloves minced garlic
- ¼  cup olive oil
- 2  tablespoons balsamic vinegar
- ¼  cup fresh finely chopped basil, stems removed (or 4 teaspoons dried basil; combine fresh and dried basil to punch up the flavor)
- ¼  teaspoon salt
- ¼  teaspoon ground black pepper
- 1  French baguette
    Fresh mozzarella slices (approximately 1 tablespoon per baguette slice)

## DIRECTIONS

1. Preheat the oven to the broiler setting.
2. In a large bowl, combine the first eight ingredients. Allow to sit 10 minutes. (This part can be made ahead and refrigerated for up to a week or frozen for several months.)
3. Cut the baguette into ¾-inch slices. On a baking sheet, arrange the slices in a single layer. Broil for 1 to 2 minutes, until slightly brown.
4. Divide the tomato mixture evenly over the baguette slices. Top with mozzarella.
5. Broil for 5 minutes or until the cheese is melted.
6. Remove from the oven and top with glow-ups, if desired (see below). Serve immediately.

*Makes 20 to 30 slices, depending on size of baguette.*


## OPTIONAL GLOW-UPS

*White truffle dark balsamic vinegar for drizzling the finished bruschetta is particularly divine if you like truffle flavor. (We use the Napastäk brand.)*

*Very thinly sliced steak (grilled, reverse seared on the smoker, or sous vide) upgrades this appetizer into a romantic dinner. Add a salad, candlelight, and smooth jazz.*

DECEMBER 8

# Joy in Giving

*Remember this—a farmer who plants only a few seeds will get a small crop.*
*But the one who plants generously will get a generous crop. You must each decide*
*in your heart how much to give. And don't give reluctantly or in response to*
*pressure. "For God loves a person who gives cheerfully." And God will generously*
*provide all you need. Then you will always have everything you need and plenty*
*left over to share with others. As the Scriptures say, "They share freely and*
*give generously to the poor. Their good deeds will be remembered forever."*

2 CORINTHIANS 9:6-9

"I DROPPED OFF K.N.'S PRESENTS TODAY, and she was so excited
opening each one! She couldn't believe how much there was, and
the foster parent couldn't stop saying how awesome this program is!
They both say a HUGE thank-you as I do! Thank you!"

I (Kendra) smiled as I read the social worker's post, knowing by
the initials that it was one of the kids we'd bought gifts for a few
weeks prior. We'd been looking for local organizations to support,
and since foster care is one area we love to focus on, this program
seemed perfect.

The idea was that you would be given a child's wish list for Christmas, along with their initials so they could remain anonymous. You would buy as many items as you would like from the list and then wrap and drop them off at a local church to be picked up and distributed by the child's social worker. When talking with our kids, we decided to ask for a boy and a girl.

Knowing that younger children often were easier to find sponsors for, I added to our request form, "Give us the older kids or whoever is hardest to place."

When we received the lists of two eighteen-year-olds, my heart broke just a little on seeing what they included. Yes, they asked for items like a particular brand of clothing, electronics, or gift cards to stores they loved. But they also asked for basic accessories like socks and underwear, things my kids wouldn't think to add to their lists because they would already be staples in their closets. Christmas gifts were things they wanted, not necessarily needed.

As we walked in and out of stores at our local mall, I explained to my kids that we wanted to be sure to get exactly what was listed to the best of our ability.

"Let's give them the best things," I reminded my children.

My kids nodded, carefully picking out items they thought the young adults would like.

"What about these, Mom?" my daughter asked, picking up a pair of shoes after searching for several minutes.

"Sure," I responded. "Do you think she'll like them?"

"I mean, I would like them," she said.

"Perfect," I said. "Put them in the cart."

We spent the next several hours ensuring we'd picked out just enough gifts for both kids.

"I think we need one more for this boy," my son said as he counted the gifts in the cart. "What about this Xbox game he's listed?"

I nodded as he made his way through the store to find it. He smiled as he brought it back and placed it with all the other items.

"Are we good with this?" I asked.

"Yeah," my kids said, smiling.

"I'd be happy with all of this," my son added.

After making all of our purchases, we went home and wrapped the presents—just as we would for anyone in our family, taking care to place the right color bow with paper, writing messages on the tags like "From a friend" and "You are loved."

A few days later, we loaded our car and drove to the drop-off site. We carried several boxes inside, greeting the workers who took our packages and thanked us. As we returned to our car, my kids asked, "That's it?" Their faces showed a little bit of a letdown that it was all over so quickly.

"Yep," I replied. "That's it. Listen, sometimes we get to see others' reactions, and sometimes we get to imagine how happy they'll be. Either way, we can trust that God is pleased with us for loving others."

They nodded as we left. A few weeks later, as I scrolled social media, I saw the organization's message and knew I needed to share it with our kids.

As we sat down to dinner that night, I read the post about the young woman who had received some of our gifts and asked, "Can you imagine what it's like to get the things on your list? And how that may be different from years past?"

My kids sat, smiling, offering their own conjectures on how it must have felt to open all the gifts. They put themselves in her position, imagining what it was like to get not just things you need but would really want as well. And they felt joy, the joy of giving, from imagining the joy the young woman must have felt. That's what I hope my kids continue to learn and remember.

There is joy in giving and in meeting the needs of another person. None of us lacks the ability to help because no matter where we find ourselves in life, we can give. Whether it's our finances, our time, our care, or our concern for others, we all have something to offer.

Scripture tells us that when we plant generously, we'll receive just as generously in return. When we sow words and actions of love, care, and compassion for others, we'll find those gifts returning to us. And once you've begun to give cheerfully, you can't help but continue because you know the blessing that comes from being a blessing to others.

If this Advent season feels stressful or lacking in joy, look around and see who may need help, whether it's a neighbor, a friend, or an organization in your community. We've not experienced the true spirit of the Christmas season more than when we've decided as a family to focus on what we can give and not just what we can get.

Even in the busiest of seasons, when we take the time to look for needs around us, in the places we already go, and with the people we already see, we'll notice ways to be a blessing to others. This isn't about adding one more thing to an already-busy time of year but about finding pockets of time to love others, just as we have been loved, and to find the deeper meaning of the season in giving out of the abundance given to us.

And when we do, we'll discover that joy is the not-so-secret by-product, as every truly generous person knows. If we allow ourselves to follow God's leading to love others, we'll leave a legacy of generosity, even if no one knows every deed we have done.

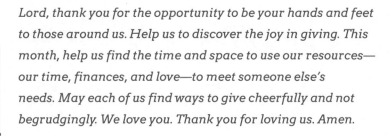

*Lord, thank you for the opportunity to be your hands and feet to those around us. Help us to discover the joy in giving. This month, help us find the time and space to use our resources— our time, finances, and love—to meet someone else's needs. May each of us find ways to give cheerfully and not begrudgingly. We love you. Thank you for loving us. Amen.*

# Reflections:

1. Read Proverbs 19:17 and Acts 20:35, and then spend a few moments reflecting on what these Scriptures mean to you. Who are you really serving when you give to others? From whom do you receive the joy and blessing of your giving?

2. Take time to pray and ask God for wisdom about those who may need your generosity. Be attentive to his nudgings about individuals or organizations as you go about your day.

3. Brainstorm practical ways that you can help someone else today. Start by thinking about the people you interact with daily—your neighbors, faith community, work, or school. What unexpected gift or act of service could brighten the season for them?

# Embracing Advent:

*Make a plan for how you can bless others in the coming days.*

# The Gift of Friendship

*The heartfelt counsel of a friend is as*
*sweet as perfume and incense.*

PROVERBS 27:9

DRAWING A DEEP BREATH to calm my nerves, I reached for the door of our local Red Lobster. I'd been invited to Girlfriend Christmas, and I was suddenly a bit bashful standing on the cusp of yet another new experience with my glittery gift bag and cute outfit. I needn't have worried though.

"Hi, Julie!" my friends warmly greeted me as I entered.

As a newlywed twentysomething, I had moved with my husband to a new community with new careers and a new church, and I was the new girl in a Tuesday afternoon Bible study meeting around Katrina's (Kendra and Kristin's sister) kitchen table.

That Bible study had started Girlfriend Christmas a year before, and what I didn't know as I crossed that doorway into Red Lobster was that this event was about to become a beloved tradition—in that form—for the next fifteen years.

Every year, we ate Cheddar Bay Biscuits, opened presents as part of our not-so-secret Santa gift exchange, posed for a photo in front of the lobster tank, visited Santa at the mall, and tried on the most ridiculous adult onesie pajamas we could find at Target. We laughed until we cried, and in the years after Katrina died, we sometimes cried until we laughed as we reminisced over funny stories and happy memories.

Girlfriend Christmas was *our* event—time and space intentionally set aside in which, over the years, we bought one another candles, chocolate, fuzzy socks, lotion, and anything else that reminded each of us that we were *seen* and *loved*. We were celebrating our friendship: a group of women who loved one another, covered one another in prayer, and showed up for one another, albeit imperfectly.

And while that version of Girlfriend Christmas has become a beloved memory that I grow a bit misty-eyed over each December, I have not let go of celebrating my female friendships in ordinary, precious ways all year long.

We've snatched moments after bedtimes for phone calls and sent video messages to one another so we can see beloved faces, no matter how many states separate us. We've piled six toddlers into the basement playroom and visited as we sat in the midst of utter (mostly happy) chaos. We've met at libraries and splash pads and on soccer field sidelines. We've manned the grill and washed the dishes at one another's parties so the hostess could focus on entertaining her guests. We've wept over one another, running to the rescue in person and in prayer. And we've rejoiced with one another, celebrating big anniversaries and successes with cake and flowers and fancy home-cooked meals.

Healthy friendships and supportive community are not the fluff of life—something lovely to be indulged in when time allows and the first to be neglected when life gets hard. They are essential to our journey, bringing joy and laughter but also encouragement and support. It's been my friends who've gently held me accountable in my marriage and my parenting, who've seen the best in me and called it out, who've told me to chase my dreams, and who've inquired whether I currently had a good work-life balance and what I was going to let go when I confessed to overwhelm.

When I think of biblical friendship, I immediately think of the relationship between Ruth and Naomi, shown in the Old Testament book of Ruth. Ruth was Naomi's daughter-in-law, and after the two of them became widowed in Moab, they journeyed back to the land of Judah, Naomi's homeland. It is a story of inconsolable grief, bitterness, anger at God, hope, faith, joy, restoration, and redemption, culminating in Ruth's marriage to Boaz and inclusion in the lineage of Jesus Christ with the birth of their son Obed.

The story of Ruth and Naomi illustrates the power of friend-ship as they filled one another's knowledge gaps, cultural expe-rience gaps, and even emotional and physical gaps. When one woman began to despair, the other was there to encourage and keep them both moving forward. They pushed and pulled one another, first back to Judah and then into survival as widowed women living there, until the entry of Boaz as the kinsman-redeemer for, ultimately, both of them. It's a gorgeous story of female friendship bridging cultures and languages, as well as a sizable age gap.

Another, less well-known image of the power of commu-nity is found in Exodus 17:8-14. During the battle against the Amalekites, Moses stood with the staff of God atop a hill overlooking Joshua as he and the Israelites fought. As long as Moses kept the staff of God raised above his head, the Israelites gained ground, but as his arms grew weary and his hands low-ered the staff, the Amalekites would advance. Aaron and Hur, seeing Moses' struggle, brought a rock for him to sit upon and, each taking an arm, kept that staff raised above his head until the battle was won by Joshua at sunset.

The ultimate success of both Ruth and Moses was only possible with the help of Naomi, Hur, and Aaron. God's plans prevailed not because of who Ruth and Moses were but because Naomi, Hur, and Aaron walked alongside them, providing emotional and physical support and lending their strength and knowledge to the situation. Ruth's and Moses' stories are but two of many in Scripture showing the importance of friendship and the strength found in healthy community.

It took me far too long to understand that friendship and community are not just a lovely, optional part of life but a powerful, essential gift from God. And each relationship is as varied and different as we are. Some relationships are only for a season based upon mutual interests, proximity, circumstance, and life stage, with others enduring decades or even entire lifetimes.

Also, as children of God, it's important to remember that sometimes we are called to be the inviters and the includers, even if we are the new ones in our neighborhood or workplace, with a cultural expectation that others will invite us.

As children of God, it's up to us to keep our circles open, asking God who he might be sending our way as we walk through church lobbies and attend the annual women's Christmas Tea instead of giving in to the comfortable temptation of sitting with the girls we already know and love.

Let's face it: strong friendships and strong community lend an extra twinkle to our Advent merriment, so let's tell our friends how much we love them with as much glitter as possible. (I'm kidding; the only thing worse than glitter is the plastic Easter grass I keep finding six months later!)

*Heavenly Father, for those struggling in friendship, we come alongside them in prayer that you will heal rifts, provide discernment about when to let go, and help them to find new, enduring friendships after moves, after major life events, and in times when it feels hard to make friends. Help us to love our friends with wild abandon, celebrating their victories as though they were our victories and mourning their losses as though they were ours. May we celebrate our friendships this Advent as the precious, spiritually powerful gifts you intended them to be. Amen.*

# Reflections:

1. Read the story of Moses, Hur, and Aaron in Exodus 17:8-14. When have you physically, spiritually, or emotionally supported a friend through what felt like an overwhelming circumstance? What specifically did that look like? How did it make you feel?

2. When has someone physically, spiritually, or emotionally supported you through what felt like an overwhelming circumstance? What specifically did that look like? How did it make you feel?

3. How are you actively keeping your circles open to new friendships God might send across your path? Consider ways you could start friendships such as sitting by someone new during Christmas parties and asking them what they are passionate about to jump-start the conversation, inviting someone you don't know well for lunch or coffee, or striking up a conversation at that cycling class or at your child's sporting event.

# Embracing Advent:

*Celebrate your friendships this Advent in ways that work for you and your friends. Small gift exchanges, an evening out, a hand-written note telling a friend how much you love her, a texted prayer over her life . . . The way you choose to celebrate is up to you!*

# A Legacy of Love

*"O death, where is your victory? O death, where is your sting?"*
*For sin is the sting that results in death, and the law gives*
*sin its power. But thank God! He gives us victory over*
*sin and death through our Lord Jesus Christ.*

I CORINTHIANS 15:55-57

THE HOLIDAYS DIDN'T FEEL RIGHT the year my sister Katrina died. Her final day was at the tail end of October, and Halloween and Thanksgiving passed in an unmemorable blur.

By the time we rounded the corner into December, Kendra and I (Kristin) and the rest of our family knew we couldn't bear to pretend that Christmas was the same. The traditions we'd loved for so long didn't fit in quite the same way, like the sister-shaped piece was missing from the puzzle box, rendering the family incomplete.

So we decided to do something new. We packed our cars and headed an hour north to a big, cozy cabin on a frozen lake. We ate bacon and cinnamon rolls for brunch at the resort lodge, swam and threw ourselves down waterslides with my young niece and nephew in the indoor pool, and gazed at the vast expanse of crystalline white snow outside the frosted windows. We threw dice and shuffled cards for board games, opened thoughtfully chosen Christmas gifts, and sat by the fireplace reading books. By the time we left, the sting of grief felt a little more bearable.

Since then, we've never fully returned to our old traditions. Instead, we've adapted them to make way for something new, keeping what worked and letting go of what didn't. It took time for us to slip into new rhythms that fit.

A friend of mine was widowed last year, just before Christmas. I was reminded, yet again, of the ongoing challenge of grief. There is the fresh grief of missing someone you love deeply. And then there's the complicated, ongoing grief of knowing that they will continue to miss all the other special moments, now and in the future— every new baby born, every wedding, every holiday—forever.

When grief threatens to steal our joy, we can find renewed strength in what remains. When it's a person that we've lost, we can honor them at Christmastime by reflecting on their legacy.

It's been almost twenty years since my sister Katrina died. Yet her legacy remains strong in us, the ones lucky to have been loved by her. She and I loved HomeGoods decor, traveling, old musicals like *Singin' in the Rain* and *Meet Me in St. Louis*, and James Taylor's music. She was also the best in the family at styling hair and clothing, had a beautiful singing voice and was part of the church's worship team, and was so personable as an executive assistant that everyone assumed she was the boss. But those characteristics only scratch the surface of who she was.

Because one of the things she truly excelled at was inviting people in. When she and her husband moved into a new neighborhood, they threw a party and invited everyone for a housewarming. She didn't wait to be asked; she created her own invitations. She frequently opened her home to others—for Bible studies, showers, parties—and fostered community. When you came to visit, her house always felt so welcoming. She'd often leave nail polish or a lotion tucked onto the dresser in the guest room when I'd stay overnight. She never overlooked small ways to make you feel loved.

So many of the things I do now, especially when offering hospitality, have been influenced by her innate ability to draw others in and make them feel important and loved. Loving others well is her legacy; someday, I want it to be mine.

When I encounter another holiday and think about missing my sister, I focus not on what I've lost but on what I've gained by knowing her.

Although we celebrate the birth of Jesus at Christmas, the hope of the Resurrection is what sustains us through the joys and sorrows of life. Because of Jesus, we have the hope of new life. As Scripture notes, death holds no sting for us since we know we'll see our loved ones again. First Thessalonians 4:13-14 reminds us that we can hold on to hope because heaven lies ahead: "We want you to know what will happen to the believers who have died so you will not grieve like people who have no hope. For since we believe that Jesus died and was raised to life again, we also believe that when Jesus returns, God will bring back with him the believers who have died."

In Jesus, we have a living hope. It's that hope that anchors our faith, sustains our souls, and gives us the courage to face each day.

One practical way to honor those we've lost is by telling others about them. For instance, on Katrina's most recent birthday, my sister Kendra, our parents, our husbands and children, and our aunt and cousin all gathered around the dining room table. With cupcakes in hand, we took turns sharing our favorite memories about Katrina.

My dad talked about how, as a child, she was always the ringleader of the group. Other kids would follow behind her in what my parents fondly referred to as "Katie's Club." We laughed about how she was voted Miss Teen Camp and reminisced about the many happy, lazy summer vacations we'd spent together at Madeline Island. Our kids were quiet, mostly, but sometimes they asked a question. None of our children ever met Katrina, but her memory is alive and well through our stories. Through laughter and tears, we've honored Katrina's legacy by inviting others to share in our memories.

When we take note of our loved ones' legacies—of love, faith and trust in God, joy, peace, or faithfulness—we can find new ways to celebrate and honor them through our traditions, old and new. At Christmastime, we can acknowledge our grief while taking comfort in the hope that we have in Jesus and the fact that until we meet our loved ones again in heaven, we can still celebrate them now. And we can feel grateful knowing that, long after we're gone, the legacy we leave in those we've loved will remain.

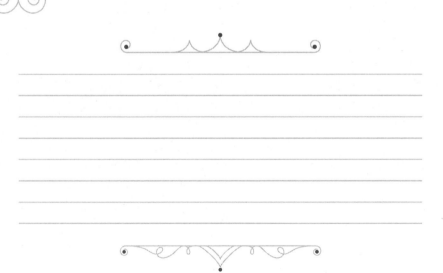

*Dear Lord Jesus, thank you for comforting us in our grief. May we hold tightly to the hope we have in you and your sustaining power to console us in every season and at every holiday. Help us find ways to celebrate and remember those no longer with us during this Christmas season, even as we gain strength from knowing we will see them again someday. Help us focus less on what we've lost and instead on everything we have gained from their legacy of love. Amen.*

## Reflections:

1. How do we honor the legacy of someone who has died? How can we honor them during the Christmas season?

2. Read Romans 12:15. Considering those around us, how can we find ways to rejoice with those who are rejoicing? In what ways can we weep with those who mourn during this season?

3. What kind of legacy are you leaving for your loved ones? If you asked them to tell you their core memories of you or characteristics you exemplify, what would they say?

## Embracing Advent:

*Reach out to a friend or loved one who is grieving in this season, and let them know you're thinking of them. Mention a specific memory of their loved one to remind them that their legacy is not forgotten. Or, if you're the one grieving a loved one, write down a few memories of them that make you smile, or share a favorite memory with a friend.*

# Good Gifts

*Whatever is good and perfect is a gift coming down to us*
*from God our Father, who created all the lights in the heavens.*
*He never changes or casts a shifting shadow. He chose to*
*give birth to us by giving us his true word. And we,*
*out of all creation, became his prized possession.*

JAMES 1:17-18

IT'S CHRISTMAS EVE.

I (Kendra) lie in bed as a young child, willing myself to sleep. I have my eyes closed and squeezed tight, believing that will somehow make me fall asleep more quickly. Turning over to my side and again to my back, I hear my younger sister's deep breathing, a clear sign she's already fallen asleep in the bed across the room. I sigh, jealous she's no longer awake.

The closet light left on with the door ajar puts a soft glow on the senior pictures of my dad still hanging on the walls of what used to be his room and sends long shadows from the well-worn

furniture he'd used as a child. After several minutes, I take a deep
breath as my heartbeat slows. My restless legs begin to still.

Downstairs, I can hear the toss of dice on a table—my parents
and grandparents playing another round of Yahtzee, their favorite
game. I'm finally lulled to sleep by the repetitive sound of the shake
and rattle of dice across the Formica tabletop that's become a familiar part of my childhood.

The next morning, I awaken, amazed that I've actually fallen
asleep. I tiptoe from my bed and peek at the clock—5:30 a.m.
*Good enough*, I think as I slowly push open the bedroom door, not
wanting the squeak of the old hinges to wake up anyone else. I
make my way down the long hallway with its white walls and its
carpet runner of muted orange, yellow, and green. I tiptoe past my
grandparents' bedroom and then my parents', where they are all
still asleep.

I turn at the end of the hallway and head down the flight of
stairs, looking toward the living room where three filled stockings
rest on the plastic-covered white couch next to the artificial tree. I
find the one with my name and smile. Taking it to the dining room
table, I turn on the TV to find cartoons and then pull each item
from the sock. I always know there will be an orange and a small
box of chocolates at the bottom, no matter what other trinkets are
included each year.

I open the candy packaging and sink my teeth into one of
the treats, saving the caramel-filled one for last. My usually strict

mother never minds us eating all our chocolates before breakfast; Christmas morning is a special occasion.

Pretty soon, my sisters and parents will be up, my dad will start the coffee, we'll have breakfast, and then we'll wait for my grandparents—especially my grandpa—to descend the stairs so we can open our gifts.

I loved Christmas as a child. It wasn't elaborate, but it always felt magical to me. Between the cozy snow-covered ground, the twinkling lights on houses and trees, the smell of cookies and treats made only this time of year, and the presents that had been lovingly wrapped and placed beneath the tree—which we'd tried for weeks to guess—it was just so special.

Now a parent myself, I want to create the same kind of excitement and tradition around Christmas morning as my parents did. We also have traditions the kids enjoy—stockings on Christmas morning, caramel rolls in the oven before anyone awakens, and the long-awaited present opening. As parents, we want to give our kids things that they desire, but the stress of being able to afford them is something I didn't know as a child would be a part of the holiday season.

And, unfortunately, I'm not alone. A recent study showed that 46 percent of adults and 53 percent of parents are worried about being able to afford gifts.[1] One of the most stressful parts about the Christmas season is wondering how we'll be able to pay for all the presents.

But the funny thing is, for as much as I remember all of our family's little traditions and quirks and my inability ever to fall asleep right away—I can't tell you what most of those gifts actually were. I'm sure my parents would laugh to hear it, knowing how much time, effort, and care they put into choosing our gifts, but I don't really remember them.

What I do remember is the feeling I had of being loved and known. My parents weren't wealthy people. Our presents weren't lavish or even expensive. But they knew me. They knew my interests and likes. And they gave me good gifts.

Maybe you, too, have struggled with the gift-giving part of Advent. Perhaps you've struggled to afford the things you know your family members want, or maybe you worry that it's too consumeristic. Too much stuff. We've had many of the same struggles in our family.

If there's anything I've taken away from my childhood, it's that my kids may not remember every gift, but they will remember the feelings they've experienced during Advent. The little traditions our family is sure to do every year, the family gatherings, the fun games. The movies and laughter. The gifts that are picked to fit their personalities and interests. It's not perfect, but we try to make it meaningful.

Just as we take care to choose presents our loved ones will like, God loves to give *us* good gifts. But not in a materialistic way that fades with tomorrow's new trend; he gives us gifts that last. Love. Joy. Peace. Mercy. Kindness.

And when we think about how Jesus came to earth to show us

just who God is and how loved we really are, we're reminded again of the greatest gift he gave—the gift of himself. The gift of his sharing in our every joy and burden.

He is the God who pursues us, who knows us, and who loves us more than anything else. Who doesn't change like a shifting shadow. Who sees us as his prized possessions.

Who surely gives good and perfect gifts.

This Advent season, let's take a lesson from our heavenly Father and give gifts to our loved ones wrapped in the things that will truly last—our love, care, and kindness. Let's find presents that are unique and convey the message that we know who our loved ones are and what will make them smile. Let's focus on making memories that will last.

*Lord, thank you for the good gifts you give to us. Help us to follow your example in the gifts that we give this Advent season. If we feel stressed, help us to find peace in you. Give us wisdom and practical ways to manage others' expectations while also making this Advent season meaningful. Give us the courage to have conversations around expectations and gift giving. Thank you for the gift of your Son and your love that is for each of us. Fill us with your peace. May we rest today, knowing we are fully known and fully loved by you. Amen.*

## Reflections:

1. Read Luke 11:9-13. Spend some time pondering these words, then make a list of the good gifts God has given to you, both the tangible and the intangible ones.

2. Do you have a favorite gift you've been given? What made it special?

3. Think about a favorite memory of Christmas with your family in the past or even recently. What made it meaningful? Based on that experience, how could you ensure lasting memories for your family in this Advent season?

## Embracing Advent:

*Have a conversation with loved ones about expectations in gift giving. Honestly share any concerns you may have and make a plan together to alleviate the stress of giving.*

# The Overlooked Main Character

*[Jesus said,] "Give, and you will receive.*
*Your gift will return to you in full—pressed down, shaken together*
*to make room for more, running over, and poured into your lap.*
*The amount you give will determine the amount you get back."*

LUKE 6:38

LOOKING AROUND THE dimly lit lower level, no one would think this was a place where anything special happened.

If you focused solely on the bare concrete floors or the brown tables lined up in rows, you'd overlook the good stuff: the piles of red and green gift bags, rolls of wrapping paper, and stacks of name tags and ribbons. You'd bypass the people chatting softly on the room's edges, faces smiling. You'd miss the joyful expectation that turned a shabby basement dressed only in a few strands of twinkling lights into a place of love and goodwill.

But with a cold blast of December air and a flurry of activity, the space was transformed. The people waiting inside hummed to life as the door flew inward, held open by a volunteer leading several children and adults inside. One by one, the volunteers raised their hands, signaling their readiness for a child to approach their table. Another volunteer would then lead a child over, garbage bag in hand, filled with bulky gift items that the table volunteer would wrap for them.

Kids Hope Shop is an annual event organized and hosted by a local shelter every December. Its purpose is to allow local at-risk kids to "shop" for their family members for free. As a volunteer, I (Kristin) have wrapped countless lotions for moms, slippers for sisters, and tool sets for uncles. I've found creative ways to wrap unwieldy basketballs for big brothers and smiled at the sight of children painstakingly laboring over labels for those they love most. I've even had a baby fall asleep in my arms while her big brother had his gifts wrapped. Some kids are somber, others wary, but all are wide-eyed with excitement over the good gifts they can't wait to share with those they love.

But the beauty of that evening isn't found in the humble surroundings or even in the gifts themselves. Instead, it's in the love demonstrated by each volunteer who emerges hours later into a starry night with aching feet and a full heart. It's in the knowledge that, as volunteers, we can be the hands and feet of Jesus, showing love through simple acts of service and participating in God's broader purpose. But what moves us to be involved in this way?

Where do we find the energy and encouragement to keep going when our feet hurt and we're ready to go home?

Perhaps we can find some answers in the Christmas narrative. When we think of this story, the main characters seem obvious: Mary, Joseph, Jesus, the shepherds, the angels, the wise men. But there's another important character who is easy to overlook: indeed, the power of the Holy Spirit is woven throughout as a guiding presence for more than one person, moving people to act and ensuring that God's purpose is fulfilled. From the beginning, it's the Holy Spirit who is named by the angel Gabriel when Mary asks how she could conceive, given that she is a virgin.

The angel explains, "The Holy Spirit will come upon you, and the power of the Most High will overshadow you. So the baby to be born will be holy, and he will be called the Son of God" (Luke 1:35). Despite what must have been an incredible and overwhelming encounter, Mary chooses to believe that what Gabriel has told her is true. She accepts that the Holy Spirit is about to move in her life in a powerful way. In Luke 1:38, Mary responds, "I am the Lord's servant. May everything you have said about me come true."

Mary's courage in believing the angel and being led by the Holy Spirit is arguably what allows the rest of the story to unfold.

Just a few days later, Mary visits Elizabeth, who is already six months pregnant with John the Baptist. Again, the Holy Spirit plays a pivotal role in bolstering their faith:

At the sound of Mary's greeting, Elizabeth's child leaped within her, and Elizabeth was filled with the Holy Spirit. Elizabeth gave a glad cry and exclaimed to Mary, "God has blessed you above all women, and your child is blessed. Why am I so honored, that the mother of my Lord should visit me? When I heard your greeting, the baby in my womb jumped for joy. You are blessed because you believed that the Lord would do what he said."

LUKE 1:41-45

The Holy Spirit causes Elizabeth to recognize how the child leaped in her womb and to offer it as an encouragement (a word that literally means to "instill courage") to Mary. Elizabeth's confidence and joy over Mary's pregnancy and her exhortation that Mary is blessed because she believed that the Lord would do what he said leads Mary to follow with her own song of praise.

When we are open to believing God and being led by the Holy Spirit, we can see glimpses of how he is moving in this world—just as Elizabeth did when her child leaped for joy within her. Elizabeth's words—directed by the Holy Spirit—provided the encouragement Mary needed to reconfirm what the angel had said.

What encouragement can we find for ourselves in these events of the Christmas story? Perhaps it is best pictured in this way: as ordinary people, we are led by the power of the Holy Spirit to believe that God will do as he said he would and will fulfill the plans he has for us.

Our response to the Holy Spirit is twofold: to believe that God's promises are true and to be moved to action because of that belief. Like Mary and Elizabeth, we are not simply bystanders in the great story God is writing throughout history—we are witnesses and participants.

As 2 Corinthians 1:21-22 reminds us, "It is God who enables us, along with you, to stand firm for Christ. He has commissioned us, and he has identified us as his own by placing the Holy Spirit in our hearts as the first installment that guarantees everything he has promised us."

Like Mary and Elizabeth, we can be encouraged by the Holy Spirit. And we can recognize how, out of the overflow of God's love for us, we can extend love to others because the power of the Holy Spirit equips and enables us to do everything God has purposed for us to do.

Though we can encourage others with our words, as Elizabeth did with Mary, we can also take another step toward serving others. Based on my own experiences at Kids Hope Shop, the physical exhaustion afterward is temporary, but the warmth and joy of helping others remains even years later.

It's a funny truth that when we serve others, our own spirits are lifted. When we give, we also receive. Scripture embodies this in a visual: "pressed down, shaken together to make room for more, running over, and poured into your lap." Science calls this a "helper's high"—the exhilarating feeling we have after we serve others. One researcher found that this joy and energy lasted several weeks and would return even when people recalled the event. A neuroscientist reported that our generosity toward someone else—whether through giving money or volunteering—activates a particular part of our brains, reinforcing feel-good neurotransmitters and making it more likely that we'll repeat the action or behavior.[1]

I love how God has wired us to want to help others! When we believe in his promises and notice the Holy Spirit at work in the world around us, we, too, can be witnesses and participants in God's great story for humanity. What a gift.

*Lord, thank you for the power of the Holy Spirit, who has been at work all along in advancing your Kingdom. Thank you for assuring us that we can believe your promises are true. Help us recognize opportunities to follow Spirit-led nudges to love and serve others well, reminding ourselves of the privilege of being the hands and feet of Jesus in this world. Amen.*

## Reflections:

1. How does our understanding of the Holy Spirit's role in the Christmas story influence how we see his power and purpose in our own lives? What can we learn from Mary's and Elizabeth's responses to the promptings of the Spirit?

2. Read Philippians 2:1-11. Following Christ's example, what are some practical ways we can demonstrate love to others and think of their needs rather than focusing solely on our own?

3. Serving benefits us as well as others. What positive outcomes have you seen in your own life as a result of serving others?

## Embracing Advent:

*Look for ways to serve others in the next week, whether through sharing a meal, donating to a local charity, or offering sincere encouragement.*

# Trading Comparison for Admiration

*Pay careful attention to your own work, for then you will get the*
*satisfaction of a job well done, and you won't need to compare yourself*
*to anyone else. For we are each responsible for our own conduct.*

GALATIANS 6:4-5

VALENTINE'S DAY OF MY OLDEST CHILD'S kindergarten year
was a shocking introduction to the world of what I (Julie) have
coined Pinterest Momming. I'd thought my daughter's store-
bought Valentines with a sucker taped to the back were cute and
fun until she came home with extravagant treat bags and carefully
crafted homemade cards from the other kids. One child had made
small piñata valentines for her classmates!

It was with a degree of disbelief and shame that I realized the
valentines I'd helped my daughter with the night before were the
simplest ones. As we surveyed her haul, it was particularly humili-
ating to hear her whisper, "My valentines are the *worst ones*!"

Of course, that was merely the beginning of my Pinterest Momming comparison problem. Elaborate 100 Days of School outfits, over-the-top leprechaun visits to ransack homes, with pots of golden candy left behind in apology . . . the Pinterest Momming waves of shame on random holidays and for unexpected reasons continually caught me by surprise during that first school year.

As a working mom whose skill sets did not (and still do not) include Elmer's glue or construction paper, it was a wild, bewildering experience. While I was accustomed to managing the lure of comparison in other areas of my life, parenting competition and comparison continue to be particularly insidious and difficult for me to manage.

If I'm not careful, Advent can easily become a Pinterest Momming nightmare of insurmountable proportions. The Christmas season is replete with shelf elves who engage in hilarious activities and might tattle to Santa, elaborate interior and exterior decor that could grace the pages of a magazine, homemade treats based on culinary-school recipes, and gorgeous photo cards arriving in a deluge starting the beginning of the month—all of which involve skill sets beyond my capabilities and each of which can easily tie me in knots as I trip headlong into the comparison trap.

As I explained my struggle with the Pinterest Momming phenomenon, a dear friend challenged me to see the situation from her perspective. She falls squarely into my definition of a Pinterest Mom, and the very things that feel like a threat or affront to my mothering are simply her way of engaging in a joy-filled expression of creativity and love. She isn't thinking about competing with my store-bought Valentines; she is fulfilling her desire to be creative in unique and life-giving ways. As a stay-at-home mom, she finds that opportunities for creative self-expression help offset her own secret fears and comparisons to working mothers.

Oh, the dangers of erroneous assumptions! My friend and I have each expended countless hours of energy fretting about how others (primarily women) view our parenting, only to find out that we had it all wrong. Of course, Pinterest, Instagram, and their ilk fan the flames of comparison and competition in quite literally every aspect of our lives. Someone is *always* doing it better than us—or that's what the professionally filtered, carefully edited message will try to tell us.

Someone will always be craftier, smarter, or better at getting children to eat beets. They will magically be traveling constantly to exotic locales, and they will never, ever have a grumpy spouse. Their on-screen lives appear close to perfection while we look up from our screen to wistfully take in the sink full of dishes and the never-diminishing pile of random paper and life detritus cluttering our kitchen table.

Comparing our secret worst to the glamour of social media is a contest stacked against us. It's in this pressure cooker of aspirational ideals versus harder-than-normal daily life that we crack. We begin to feel like we are the only ones struggling while everyone around is joyous 24-7 and doing all the things with no bickering, no crying, and no missteps.

Let's jump off the aspirational bandwagon of false expectations—at Christmas and beyond—in every way and as soon as possible. And let's keep jumping off as often as we need to. As today's verse reminds us, focusing on the joy of what we're doing, without concern for who is *certainly* doing it differently or better, keeps us rooted in present contentment.

And that's where I long to be.

I want to enjoy the lopsided, two-trunked, real tree my family intentionally dragged home because we momentarily felt sorry for it.

I want to find my box of mismatched tree ornaments as beautiful as they are sentimental, despite the hilarious, tacky ones I love, the homemade ones toted home from preschool, and the utter lack of any theme, color or otherwise.

I want my family to respond to the potatoes spilled just as they were pulled from the oven with warm hugs and comforting words, along with some gentle laughter and teasing tossed around by the end of the meal about "if only we'd had potatoes . . ."

Can we let go of striving (however that looks to us personally) and simply enjoy, including embracing the times that are a bit rough in the moment but can be laughed about later? Spreading Christmas cheer is not a competition. And my role in bringing heaven to earth during this season *should* look different from yours.

If God created us as unique individuals with different skills, love languages, and circles of friends (and he did!), it stands to reason that what brings contentment, beauty, and joy to me is going to be different from what brings those feelings to you. I can find contentment in my unique giftings and skill sets and still sincerely appreciate, admire, and wholeheartedly applaud your giftings and skill sets without falling into the vortex of comparison.

Let's give one another the gift of unconditional admiration this Christmas as we enjoy how others make Advent merrier and brighter in their own unique ways.

*Heavenly Father, thank you for the infinite variations of creativity you've poured out among us. Thank you for expressions of joy as unique and individual as we are. Help us to recognize the collective beauty of our creativity rather than agonizing over the vicious cycle of who does what better than we do. May we be people who celebrate and appreciate the God-given creativity in one another rather than constantly measuring ourselves against it. Amen.*

# Reflections:

1. Read Psalm 139:13-16. What does remembering that God knew us as individuals, forming our bodies in the womb, reveal about comparing our secret worst moments and selves to the public best of others?

2. In what areas are you prone to comparison, either feeling ashamed or less than others or feeling prideful and better than those around you? Reread today's verses (Galatians 6:4-5). Why are both forms of comparison dangerous?

3. Are there specific online platforms that fan the flames of comparison rather than simply encouraging or inspiring you? If so, how can you better manage their influence?

# Embracing Advent:

*Make two lists. For the first one, list your skills, giftings, passions, and talents. Ask two trusted people to make a similar list about you. Add whatever they say onto your list without disputing it. Ask God to use each item for his glory.*

*For your second list, give someone else a list of three things that you've noticed she is good at, including a prayer that God would continue to use her in those areas.*

DECEMBER 14

# God's Promises Are True

*One generation shall commend your works to another,*
*and shall declare your mighty acts.*

PSALM 145:4, ESV

THE ONLY GENETIC TRAIT I (Kristin) was sure my kids would have was blue eyes. Since all four grandparents have blue eyes—both my parents and my husband's parents—and my husband and I have blue eyes, it seemed likely. My memories of sixth-grade science and Mendelian genetics are fuzzy, but I'm pretty sure that is how DNA works.

Although my children did emerge with blue eyes, they also possess traits I didn't expect, like my husband's sense of humor, my slow-burn temper, my husband's love of entertaining, and my love of books. Both the characteristics that cause me great delight and those that provoke the urge to roll my eyes in exasperation can be seen in my daughters and their unique personalities.

Just as I've passed traits to my children, I've received characteristics from my parents. I've got my mom's gentleness and my dad's
optimism. And I'll gladly blame my love of sugar on my dad's self-
described Norwegian sweet tooth.

I'm fascinated by families and the characteristics they display,
including those in the story of Zechariah and, later, his son John
the Baptist. Technically, John the Baptist's birth occurs just before
the Christmas story. But when we consider the scope of history, it's
essential to consider what came before and what came afterward.

The first chapter of Luke tells us that Zechariah and his wife,
Elizabeth, are a childless couple who are both descended from
priestly lines. They are "righteous in God's eyes, careful to obey all
of the Lord's commandments and regulations" (Luke 1:6).

One day, while Zechariah is serving at the Temple, burning
incense in the sanctuary, an angel of the Lord appears to him.
Though he is afraid, the angel reassures him and gives him the
startling news that his wife, Elizabeth, will have a son. According
to the angel, the son will be filled with the Holy Spirit and will
serve with a spirit and power like the great prophet Elijah,
preparing people for the coming of the Lord and turning their
hearts to God.

At this point, Zechariah expresses some doubts. "How can I be
sure this will happen?" he asks. After all, he and his wife are both
beyond childbearing age.

The angel responds by admonishing him for not believing what he has heard about God's plans and tells him that because of his doubt, he won't be able to speak aloud until the child is born.

Several months later, after the child's birth, neighbors and relatives assemble for the circumcision ceremony. They assume the child's name will be Zechariah, after his father. When Elizabeth counters that his name will be John, the others are astounded by the decision to use a nonfamily name, and they ask Zechariah to confirm or deny it. After motioning for something to respond with, he writes, "His name is John." Instantly, his speech returns, and he praises God.

What I love about this story—besides the fact that this couple conceived after waiting so long—is what it reveals about how God deals with our doubts. He doesn't shame Zechariah, but he does respond by silencing him.

Gabriel declares, "Since you didn't believe what I said, you will be silent and unable to speak until the child is born. For my words will certainly be fulfilled at the proper time" (Luke 1:20).

Is this temporary inability to speak a punishment, or is it actually an invitation to ponder quietly in the presence of the Lord? What else can account for Zechariah's transformation from someone who argues with the angel to someone who offers a beautiful song of praise to the Lord?

Sometimes, our words reveal the limits of our understanding of God's purposes. On the other hand, silence can invite us to quiet our hearts and minds. Rather than focusing on the limitations our words reveal, we leave space in our silence that God can fill.

Because by the time Zechariah writes that his son's name is John, he has been changed. And the experience reminds us that God is always and already at work. He doesn't need us to agree; his power is already working.

Years later, the doubt that once tripped up Zechariah would materialize again in his son, John. Just as the angel had prophesied, John had a vibrant ministry. He had followed in his parents' footsteps and—as befits their priestly lineage—had been set apart from birth, preparing the way for Jesus.

Jesus was a relative of John the Baptist. Though we have no anecdotal evidence of any interaction between John and Jesus during the thirty years before Jesus' ministry began, I wonder if that family connection influenced John. After all, I still remember when my mischievous cousin told me that the electric fencing at their farm was turned off and dared me to touch it. It wasn't off, and that quick zap landed me on my rear end in the grass and taught me to take my cousin's word with a grain of salt. Perhaps, in a similar way, John wondered if someone who was his peer and relative could truly be the Savior.

Yet by the time John and Jesus connected during Jesus' ministry, John seemed convinced that his kinsman was indeed the Son of God. He even baptized Jesus in the Jordan River and triumphantly shouted, "Look! The Lamb of God who takes away the sin of the world!" (John 1:29).

But later, as he is imprisoned and awaiting death, the doubts creep in.

He asks his disciples to go to Jesus and pose this question: "Are you the Messiah we've been expecting, or should we keep looking for someone else?" (Matthew 11:3).

There's so much pain and vulnerability in that question. It's one we can find ourselves asking when a loved one dies, bad things happen to good people, or injustice occurs. *Jesus, are you really who you say you are?*

Just like his father, Zechariah, John is questioning God's plan. But though Zechariah was challenged with silence by the angel, Jesus' response is different. He doesn't silence John. Instead, he answers, "Go back to John and tell him what you have heard and seen—the blind see, the lame walk, those with leprosy are cured, the deaf hear, the dead are raised to life, and the Good News is being preached to the poor. . . . God blesses those who do not fall away because of me" (Matthew 11:4-6).

In other words, Jesus' response to John echoes the essence of the angel's response to Zechariah: *God's promises are being fulfilled. Is that not the proof you need?*

I'm encouraged by the idea that Zechariah and John, who came from generations of faithful men and women, still experienced doubt. And that God met them not with scorn or derision but with compassion and what they needed: for Zechariah, a silence that created space for God to fill; for John, an answer that got to the heart of why we wrestle with our faith.

Perhaps you've experienced seasons of doubt. Sometimes, when we watch friends and loved ones struggle with addiction or loss, chronic pain, financial problems, or marital woes, we can struggle to see God's goodness in those circumstances. Though we can't always envision the ending from where we are, God can. He's not thrown off by our doubts or worried by our circumstances.

Not all of us have earthly fathers or mothers to emulate, but we all have a heavenly Father whose lead we can follow. He wants to give us a rich spiritual heritage of joy, peace, and contentment. The Psalms remind us that from generation to generation we can share about God's greatness—his mighty acts, and how he's loved us so well. When we choose to trust God and his promises, we can create new pathways for those who follow behind us to tread. Believing God's promises provides the roots of faithfulness we need for developing a rich spiritual heritage for our children or others we mentor.

*Heavenly Father, thank you that you don't scorn our doubts. Though your answers may not be what we want, they are what we need. Help us to see your fingerprints revealed even in circumstances where they feel hidden. Thank you that we can trust you and that you keep your promises. May we build upon the foundation of your truth as we trust in you. Amen.*

## Reflections:

1. Is there any circumstance that is currently causing you to question God's goodness? Is there an area of your life in which you are unable to foresee a good outcome?

2. Read Exodus 14:14 and Psalm 141:3. What do these verses tell us about silence and wisdom? How can we incorporate those ideas into our prayer time with God or our daily interactions with others?

3. How can you, like Zechariah, claim God's goodness? (Read Zechariah's words of praise in Luke 1:68-79 if you need ideas.)

## Embracing Advent:

*On a sticky note, write down three situations in your life in which God kept his promises. Find a prominent place—on your mirror, bedside table, or fridge—to post your note as a reminder of his faithfulness.*

# Vanilla Almond Rolls

*I first got this recipe from my mom after she'd made it one Christmas morning. It started a tradition in our house as well that my kids continue to ask for every year. There's just something about waking up to the sweet smell of baked goods ready to eat after opening presents. But please note: although easy, this recipe does need to be assembled the night before you want to bake it.*

## INGREDIENTS

- 1 teaspoon almond extract
- ½ cup butter
- 1 cup firmly packed brown sugar
- 18 frozen dinner rolls (we use Rhodes)
- ¼ cup sliced almonds
- 1 package cook-and-serve vanilla pudding mix (*not* instant)

## DIRECTIONS

1. In a small glass bowl, microwave almond extract, butter, and brown sugar on high for one minute. Stir. Microwave an additional minute until bubbly.
2. Spray or grease a Bundt pan.
3. Place frozen dinner rolls in the pan, layering as needed, and pour the sugar mixture over them evenly.
4. Sprinkle with almonds and dry pudding mix.
5. Cover with plastic wrap and let rise overnight. (Grease plastic wrap before placing over rolls so it doesn't stick.)
6. Bake 25 to 30 minutes at 350 degrees Fahrenheit until golden brown.
7. Remove from oven and cool 10 minutes before removing from pan. Serve warm.

*Makes 9 to 12 servings.*

DECEMBER 15

# When Advent Isn't Perfect

*Repay no one evil for evil, but give thought to*
*do what is honorable in the sight of all. If possible,*
*so far as it depends on you, live peaceably with all.*

ROMANS 12:17-18, ESV

"I JUST DON'T KNOW if I can do it, Kendra," a close friend con-
fided to me over coffee one brisk December morning. Nestled
next to a burning fireplace in the corner of a local coffee shop,
my friend shared her heart. "I feel bad, and honestly, we don't
talk to anyone else about this because I'm embarrassed and
a little ashamed."

She looked up at me shyly, assessing whether she should go on.
I gave a little smile, and she continued. "I just don't know if I want
to spend a lot of time with my family over the holidays. It creates
so much anxiety in me."

I nodded in understanding. "I think more people out there feel the same way. And you're right—it's not something we talk about often, but many people experience stress in family relationships."

Over the next hour, we discussed her complicated family history and the relationships that were still somewhat strained, albeit mainly below the surface.

"It'd be different if we could talk about things that have happened," she continued, "but everyone just wants to sweep it under the rug. For years, I just went along, but I don't want to do that anymore—not with having my own kids now."

"It definitely complicates things," I agreed. "And you have a right to your feelings and wanting some healthy boundaries. But . . . do you want to see them, even just for a bit?"

She cocked her head to the side, contemplating. "I do," she said.

"So, what would you be willing to do?" I asked, and we brainstormed times she could get together while also giving herself and her family a way out if things went awry.

"That all sounds good," I said as we wrapped up our time together, "but before we go, can we just acknowledge the sadness of the situation? The unmet expectations and the desire that's there for something different? Something more healthy and whole?"

She nodded as tears began to fill our eyes and then spill down our cheeks, unchecked.

As we embraced and prayed together for God's continued wisdom and peace over the situation, I knew her struggle wasn't over. Relationships can be messy and complicated, and the holidays don't change that. In fact, at times, they can magnify the issues.

I know this all too well. Being a foster and adoptive mom, I've had a front-row seat to complicated, messy relationships between family members. Even when people mean well and genuinely love their family, they can still cause hurt or continue in unhealthy patterns that have become habits over time.

For one of our kids, the problem isn't just the relationships; the holidays themselves don't elicit many warm, fuzzy memories. She doesn't have the traditions or happy memories that many families do, which means that she'd rather avoid holidays altogether. Even today, she struggles to participate and will opt out of family holiday get-togethers by working a shift as a way to avoid them.

So, what do we do if we have strained relationships or know others who do but aren't sure how to help them? What about our unmet expectations, whether from our younger years or even today? Here are three steps we can take to find healing:

1. *We acknowledge the unhealthiness or unmet expectations and allow ourselves to be honest about what has happened or continues to persist.* Within that, we let ourselves grieve what is not and what we wish could be. We may need to set boundaries with

others so that we can have peace of mind. Family members aren't granted an all-access pass to our lives simply because they are related to us.

2. *We always bring our heartache to God.* He sees. He knows. He understands. There is no shame in telling him about our pain. When we do, we can trust that he will comfort us. First Peter 5:7 says that we can give every worry and care to God, because he cares about us.

3. *We find someone we can trust to confide in.* Healing comes when we allow someone else to witness our pain and when we allow someone to offer wisdom and comfort. Someone who will pray with us and remind us of who we are in Christ. Someone who will hold our stories in confidence. Someone we can trust.

   Oftentimes, we may not share because we worry that we are doing something wrong, but this isn't the same as going around gossiping or continuing to speak ill of others to anyone and everyone who will listen. This is about finding a person who is safe and who will offer support, another perspective, and wisdom when you need it.

As my kids have grown, we've shifted boundaries with family members, sometimes allowing more contact and other times pulling back based on the needs of our kids and the way their family members are interacting with them. There is no perfect way to do relationships. And we may make mistakes as well. That's okay.

Some may wonder if boundaries are Christlike, but today's Scripture tells us that *as much as it depends on us*, we are to live at peace with others. This lets us know that we are not responsible for others' actions or behavior, nor can we control anyone else but ourselves. If others act in ways that aren't loving, boundaries are a way to live at peace without allowing others to harm us.

Grief during the holidays is normal and even expected. Whether it's grief over unmet expectations or troubled relationships, we can be sure that God sees and knows our pain. We can enter the Advent season believing there is good to be found, even when sorrow is also present, and they often run in tandem with one another. We can be fully joyful and fully grieved all at the same time. We don't have to trade one for the other.

Advent is for all of us, so come to Jesus in this season, no matter what situation you find yourself in. In him you are fully known and fully loved—you and every bit of your past, present, and future story.

Joy and peace, even celebration, can be experienced in this season. So set boundaries where needed, create new traditions for yourself and your family, engage in pursuits that encourage your faith, and be merry in all that is good.

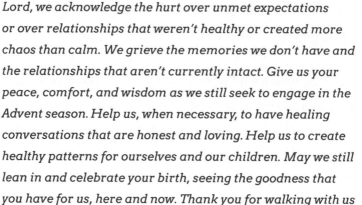

*Lord, we acknowledge the hurt over unmet expectations or over relationships that weren't healthy or created more chaos than calm. We grieve the memories we don't have and the relationships that aren't currently intact. Give us your peace, comfort, and wisdom as we still seek to engage in the Advent season. Help us, when necessary, to have healing conversations that are honest and loving. Help us to create healthy patterns for ourselves and our children. May we still lean in and celebrate your birth, seeing the goodness that you have for us, here and now. Thank you for walking with us through the good and challenging parts of this Advent. We love you. Amen.*

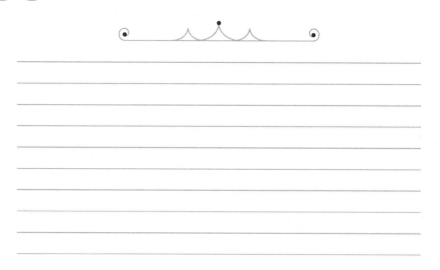

## Reflections:

1. Read Psalm 34:18. Spend some time pondering what this verse means to you. How do you sense God's nearness to you in this Advent season?

2. Do you have relationships or life circumstances that have unmet expectations attached to them or that are causing some other stress or strain? Based on the steps outlined above, how could you adjust your approach to find healing?

3. Are there boundaries you need to put into place to give yourself or those around you more peace during this season?

## Embracing Advent:

*Allow yourself to grieve what is not perfect while also thanking God for the good that is there. Be honest with him about the situation while praying for healing and wisdom to engage in a way that allows you to live at peace with those around you. If possible, seek out someone you could confide in about your circumstances.*

# Recalibrating with God

*Be still, and know that I am God! I will be honored by*
*every nation. I will be honored throughout the world.*

PSALM 46:10

*UGH. I HATE THIS.*

My house was silent, and it was far later into the night than I
had intended to be awake. Sitting in the soft glow of our Christmas
tree, a cup of tea in hand, I studied my list for how December was
*supposed* to go. Skimming over all the tasks that should already have
been done, activities that felt more burdensome than cheery and fun,
projects I could not do with the flawless execution of those around
me, I heaved a weary sigh of frustrated sadness.

*Julie, will you ever get this right?* I asked myself. *Why are your*
*good intentions always at least two sizes too big for the chaotic run-up*
*to Christmas?*

Yet again, I had overestimated the time and energy my family had available while vastly underestimating obligations from school, work, church, and family, which—while enjoyable—are unmovable calendar fixtures requiring everything else to flex around them during the countdown toward Christmas.

Shaking myself out of self-recrimination before I started to spiral further, I recounted the fun things, the *good* things, the obligations I'd already met. Then I took to God the items yet to be done, stilling my body and mind as I turned to Scripture, prayerfully asking him to help me reorder my list in light of our remaining time and in alignment with his will.

After that silent pause followed by prayer, I tucked my favorite tea mug, now empty, into the dishwasher and trundled off to bed, determined to reevaluate everything in the morning after sleep and further prayer.

That late-night moment happens year after year. I have never figured out the perfect balance for December and am starting to suspect that it is an illusion. Instead of beating myself up for exuberant planning, I am learning to prayerfully recalibrate each mid-month by stilling myself in God's presence, seeking which activities are a priority and which need to be released for this year, for this phase of life, or forever.

It is a challenge to quiet myself before God any time of the year, but that challenge is magnified in the whirlwind known as Advent. Yet it is in that intentional stillness that he is honored and that he can speak into our hearts, minds, and spirits. In those moments, I find encouragement and peace, and I arrive at a revised list better aligned with God's purposes.

Here are questions I prayerfully take before God about my Christmas to-do lists:

1. *What items on my list are eternally significant versus those that have value but are not focused on the eternal?* While embracing just-for-fun traditions of all kinds is important, centering the gift of Jesus' birth and acting as his hands and feet is our cornerstone.

2. *What traditions have I fallen into because of expectation or obligation rather than joy or intentional choice?* Can I outsource, reduce, or remove any or all of them? For example, after years of stressed-out baking, I now purchase my Christmas cookies and send Christmas cards every other year. Now that my kids are teenagers, these changes create a more peaceful December because I have outsourced activities that are more stressful than fun for my family. Of course, you may love baking and sending Christmas cards, but you hate the idea of hunting for a real Christmas tree—something we love. Our lists of what to keep and what to let go of may be completely different!

3. *When is "good enough" the appropriate standard versus a temptation toward perfection?* Can some presents be in gift bags rather than wrapped? Could outdoor decor be minimized even

as you go all out inside? Can a gathering be held in January rather than December to ease everyone's schedules? Is there part of the Christmas Eve dinner that can be catered rather than prepared from scratch? Can presents for extended family be turned into a new tradition of volunteering together to serve a meal at a shelter? What tasks can a spouse or children take on in which the results are appreciated and praised without requiring redoing or correction?

4. *Which items incorporate values of giving and gratitude as a core part of the experience?* The most successful way we have found to push back against the commercial aspects of Christmas is to embrace opportunities to give and thank.

5. *Are there items on my list because I strive to "keep up with the Joneses" rather than doing Advent in a way that fits my life or family?* What works for your friends, family, coworkers, or neighbors may not work for you and your family, and that is okay! Without diminishing their approach, embrace what works for you and let go of those things meant only to keep up appearances.

These are questions I ask myself based on my own tendencies to stray from God's best. They are meant simply as a starting point for your own analysis. As you still yourself before God, your questions and convictions will be based on your stage of life, the people in your household, and the community you live in. As you recalibrate with God throughout Advent, you can find your way back to merry and bright together.

*Heavenly Father, you are sovereign over heaven and earth, and you are worthy of honor from every nation and every people group! Amid the hustle and bustle of this season, the sacredness of our Savior's birth can get a bit lost; forgive us for our distraction and draw us back to you. Take our to-do lists, obligations, and traditions and reorder them to match your will and Kingdom. Restore us to an appropriate balance as we seek to honor you amid the expectations placed on us. May we bring heaven to earth, revealing your love for the world as we move through these days. Amen.*

# Reflections:

1. Read Isaiah 9:2, 6-7. Nothing about the Nativity story was happenstance. The birth of Christ was foretold hundreds of years in advance. In what ways does a glimpse of the master plan help you recalibrate during Advent?

2. Is there a question or consideration unique to you and your circumstances that you would add, change, or subtract from the list in today's reading?

3. Based on the questions in the reading, how could you recalibrate your to-do lists and obligations? Spend five (or more!) minutes in prayerful reflection, reading Scripture and thanking God for as many things as you can list.

# Embracing Advent:

*After asking God for wisdom, recalibrate your calendar, your to-do lists, and your obligations. Commit to a prayerful weekly check-in with him. Embrace those moments of connection over a cup of coffee or tea, in a place that invites peaceful reflection.*

# ℛecognizing Jesus

*Fix your thoughts on what is true, and honorable, and right, and*
*pure, and lovely, and admirable. Think about things that are excellent*
*and worthy of praise. . . . Then the God of peace will be with you.*

PHILIPPIANS 4:8-9

RECENTLY, I (Kristin) heard about the idea of a "glimmer." Coined
by a licensed clinical social worker named Deb Dana, who special-
izes in complex trauma, this term refers to small moments when
we feel connected or regulated. It's the opposite of a "trigger," and
instead of causing a painful memory to surface, a glimmer cues our
nervous system to feel calm and safe. It's a moment that makes us
feel hopeful, joyful, happy, or grateful.[1]

Our brains have often been trained to look for the bad, which
is understandable since we want to prepare for what could happen
and assess threats or difficulties as they arise. But while it's essential to plan ahead, sometimes it's too easy to focus solely on what's

going wrong. Retraining our brains to look for the good takes time and effort. The remarkable thing about our brains is that, thanks to neuroplasticity—the ability to create new pathways—the more we practice looking for good things, the more quickly our brains will recognize them.

It shouldn't surprise us that the science behind glimmers echoes what Scripture tells us. After all, when Paul admonishes us to focus on what is true, honorable, lovely, and admirable, it's a reminder that doing so cultivates peace. And when we stop to consider the "micro-moments" of glimmers in our lives, we'll begin to notice how frequently they arrive. Perhaps it's the steam rising from a cup of coffee, the few moments of silence before anyone else is awake, or the crackle of a wooden-wick candle that smells like balsam and cedar or black cardamom and vanilla (my personal favorite). Maybe it's the brisk, bracing outdoor air that makes our lungs expand or hearing our favorite Christmas tune as we wheel a cart through the grocery store. Perhaps it's the satisfaction of smoothing the edges of gift wrap or getting the crease just right, placing a gift we know someone will love under the tree, drinking creamy eggnog poured into a chilled glass, or sinking into a piping hot bath on a chilly day. It could be the warm presence of a child who curls up next to us for a Hallmark movie, watching the flickering flames from a fire, seeing the twinkle of lights on the tree, or admiring bright stars glittering across the dark expanse of the sky on a moonlit night.

None of those moments are earth-shattering by themselves, but when we consider them all together, they add up to a beautiful day and they help to smooth the rough edges of a hectic holiday season.

For me, glimmers are not simply things that bring me joy but small reflections of the love of Jesus. It's his light that illuminates the world. When we notice these tiny glimpses of beauty, do we recognize him as the source? Do we thank him for these small reminders of his love?

In Luke 2, we read about two people named Simeon and Anna who were both highly attuned to noticing glimpses of the Lord. Both individuals had lived a long time in service to the Lord, and they were eagerly awaiting the Messiah. Their greatest desire was to see the Savior. Scripture notes that Simeon was a righteous man, and the Holy Spirit had revealed to him that he wouldn't die until he saw the Messiah. Anna, too, had waited a long time to meet the promised Redeemer. As a prophet, she had spent decades in the Temple, waiting and worshiping God with fasting and prayer.

On the day that Mary and Joseph brought the infant Jesus to the Temple, they were approached first by Simeon and then by Anna. Simeon had followed the Holy Spirit's lead by being present at the Temple that day, and when he saw Jesus, Simeon took him in his arms and began to praise God: "Sovereign Lord, now let your servant die in peace, as you have promised. I have seen your salvation, which you have prepared for all people. He is a light to reveal God to the nations, and he is the glory of your people Israel!" (Luke 2:29-32).

In Jesus, Simeon's hope was fulfilled. Only in Jesus is the fullest depiction of the love of God revealed—the light of salvation, available to all people. Jesus is the culmination of the promises of God.

Just as Jesus and his parents were talking to Simeon, they were approached by Anna. Immediately, she praised God and shared the good news with others as she "talked about the child to everyone who had been waiting expectantly for God to rescue Jerusalem" (Luke 2:38).

Simeon and Anna were witnesses to the good news of Jesus' birth. Their attitude of joyful expectancy allowed them to be open to the Holy Spirit's leading and to recognize the Savior of the world in the face of an infant. Instead of questioning why Jesus had not arrived as a powerful king or ruler, they rejoiced in his presence. They recognized Jesus because they were looking for him.

Though Jesus no longer walks among us physically, when we stay in close relationship to him and follow the Spirit's lead, we, too, can recognize the work of Jesus in the world. Every glimmer of love and hope—even the tiny ones that arise throughout our days—leads back to him, and when we are intentional about noticing those glimmers, we bear witness to his work in the world. You and I become witnesses and participants in the good work of God and his Kingdom. What a privilege.

Though Jesus is the Light of the World (see John 8:12), he asks us to reflect the glimmers of his light and love toward others. He told his followers in Matthew 5:14-16,

> You are the light of the world—like a city on a hilltop that cannot be hidden. No one lights a lamp and then puts it under a basket. Instead, a lamp is placed on a stand, where it gives light to everyone in the house. In the same way, let your good deeds shine out for all to see, so that everyone will praise your heavenly Father.

Let's watch for the glimmers in our day that help us to walk out of the darkness and into his light. Then let's reflect those glimpses of God's goodness to others. As God's children, we are the world's light, shining out for all to see. Let's not allow the world to dim the glimmer but act as sparks that light a fire in our souls.

*Dear Jesus, thank you for the small moments in our day that remind us of your love, grace, compassion, and mercy. Help us reflect your light into the world so that others may know you. May we always focus on what is true, honorable, right, pure, lovely, admirable, and worthy of praise. Help us to retrain our brains to see the good and, as we do, to find new ways to partner with you in demonstrating your love and kindness to others. Amen.*

## Reflections:

1. Have you ever heard of the concept of "glimmers"? In what ways could focusing on such tiny moments of safety and comfort change your outlook on life?

2. Simeon and Anna were joyfully expectant that God's promises would be fulfilled in their lifetimes. Do you feel like the same is true for you? Why or why not? How could you shift your attitude to one of joyful expectation as you intentionally seek out glimpses of Jesus' love in your life?

3. Read Romans 12:9. How can choosing to "hold tightly to what is good" influence how we love others?

## Embracing Advent:

*Using a piece of paper or a notes app, keep track of glimmers today as you notice them. Then, thank God for them.*

# ℞econsidering the Innkeeper

*She gave birth to her firstborn son. She wrapped him
snugly in strips of cloth and laid him in a manger,
because there was no lodging available for them.*

LUKE 2:7

AS I (JULIE) HAVE READ AND reread the story of Jesus' birth and
the intentionally humble way he intersected our world in human
form, I have grown curious about the unnamed side characters,
including the innkeeper. For most of my life, I have disdained the
anonymous innkeeper in the Christmas story. He is forever "that
guy"—the one whose lack of room for a heavily pregnant, teenage
Mary meant Jesus was born among livestock.

When I was a young girl, I mentally classified the innkeeper as
greedy, callous, and uncaring for not opening a room in the inn
for sweet Baby Jesus. (How dare he!?) Somehow, that childhood
irritation followed me into adulthood, unexamined: condemning

and unforgiving. It was not until recently that I reexamined my unyielding dislike for this unnamed soul who played a pivotal role in the Nativity story.

Did you know that the innkeeper is never actually mentioned in Scripture? Today's verse is the only one we get about Jesus' birth accommodations, which means we've built our perceptions of the innkeeper on one solitary verse.

Let us reconsider the Nativity story from his perspective through questions (while being exceptionally careful about filling in the gaps with fictional imaginings): How many times had Mary and Joseph been turned away before arriving at the innkeeper's doorstep? Did he offer space among his animals, and if so, was it compassion that moved him to aid them, or was it a commercial transaction? Did he (or others staying there) assist and offer supplies as Mary went into labor? When did he hear about the angels appearing to the shepherds and directing them to the infant Jesus? Was he present during that chaotic commotion? Did he realize or even wonder—this side of heaven—that he had met the Son of God?

Of course, no one alive today knows the answers to those questions, but they have made me reevaluate my assumptions and rethink my own efforts to be the hands and feet of Jesus.

What if, instead of assuming him stingy and gruff, we assumed the best of that innkeeper? I've had to ask forgiveness for my hard-hearted view of him over my lifetime. Maybe he was the pseudo-villain of my young imagination, but perhaps he was a God-fearing man doing the best he could with what he had available, unaware that his Savior's imminent arrival would take place among his animals. What if he was generous with what he had left during the rooms-sold-out-all-over-town census, knowing it was deeply imperfect but better than the alternative of turning them away?

*Uffda.* If that pokes a tender spot in your spirit, please know you are not alone! It's convicting to wonder whether I've spent a lifetime condemning a man who gave the best of what he had in that moment of extreme accommodation scarcity.

And, more distressing, I contemplate the times I've fallen short of what the innkeeper offered. How many times has Jesus sent someone across my path, and I chose not to help, convinced that what I had to offer wasn't good enough so I shouldn't bother trying? Or what about those instances in which I've refused to help because it was inconvenient? And I know there have been times of obliviousness in which I was too distracted to recognize the opportunity to be a part of the God Story in someone else's life.

It is possible I have carried disdain for a person who answered the call of God more faithfully than I have thus far.

What do we do when we come face-to-face with our inadequacies, our sinful selfishness, and our hypocrisy?

*We repent.* We take our obliviousness, our self-centeredness, our fear, and our insecure certainty that we have nothing worthwhile to offer, and we lay all of it at the feet of Jesus. We confess the times we know we got it wrong, and we confess the distractions in our life that cause obliviousness. Proverbs 28:13 reminds us that confronting and confessing our sins leads to mercy.

*We accept forgiveness.* Instead of wallowing in self-loathing and contempt for the ways we've fallen short, we embrace the forgiveness that comes with repentance. And then, when God removes our sin as far as the east is from the west, we also let it go (see Psalm 103:12). We do not stay stuck in a vortex of self-recrimination and guilt.

*We seek a second chance.* Scripture is full of stories about fresh starts and second chances, and we are in good company with the likes of Saul, who consented to the murder of Stephen and persecuted early Christians, yet encountered the resurrected Jesus on the road to Damascus. We now know him as Paul, the author of at least thirteen books in the New Testament (see Acts 9:1-19). If a murderer can become the primary biographer of the early church and the most prolific author in the New Testament, then there is nothing we have done in life that places us beyond the redemptive power of God.

*We reevaluate.* What in our life hinders our ability to love God with our entire heart, soul, and mind? What keeps us from loving others as we love ourselves? What skill sets, talents, experiences, and resources can we use to love God and others? The answers will look different as we move through seasons and stages in our lives, but intentional reflection on a regular basis helps us course correct when we start to slip into old patterns.

And finally, *we entrust our small offerings to God's infinite wisdom and plan and align ourselves with him* rather than asking him to bless our plans done our way. There is zero doubt that God intended for the Savior of all humanity to be born in the humblest of accommodations. Regardless of whether the innkeeper was a devout follower or a greedy villain, God used him to accomplish his will.

We are called to obedience, which means we do not substitute our judgment, our plans, or ourselves for God. We are generous with what God has entrusted to us and watchful and willing as he invites us into his story, in his timing, and in his way. Aligning ourselves with God's will is the best way to ensure a merry and bright Advent, this year and forever.

*Heavenly Father, forgive us for our obliviousness, our distraction, and our hard-hearted ways. May we see people as you see them. May we encounter the world through the lens of Jesus' teachings. And may we practice prayerful obedience rather than substituting our judgment for yours. Thank you for redemption, for second chances, and for opportunities to be used by you to accomplish your will in the lives around us and in the world. Amen.*

# Reflections:

1.  Read Luke 10:25-28, the great commandment. In what ways does your life reveal that you are loving God with all your heart, soul, strength, and mind? Are there areas where you are stubbornly asking God to bless what you have decided to do without prayerful input from him?

2.  Read Luke 10:29-37. What prevents you from loving your "neighbors"? Is it distractions, inconvenience, fear, or something else? Write down what comes to mind.

3.  Pray over the list you made in question two. How can you become a more responsive partner with God as he seeks people who will serve as his hands and feet?

# Embracing Advent:

*Pick one list item you prayed over in question 3 and ask God for a second chance. What can you do today to better align with God on this item? What do you need to do to consistently align with God on this for twenty-one days (the time it takes to form a new habit)?*

# Seasons of Grace

*The Lord will guide you continually, giving you water*
*when you are dry and restoring your strength. You will be*
*like a well-watered garden, like an ever-flowing spring.*

ISAIAH 58:11

"HURRY UP!" I CALLED TO MY HUSBAND. "We're going to be late. I told everyone we'd be there at noon."

"Coming, Kendra!" he called from upstairs. I watched him carry our young son, crying and kicking his little legs, down the stairs. "It's okay. You'll have time to play with your toys later," he said soothingly.

As we buckled the kids in and pulled out of the drive, hurrying to make it to an extended family gathering that Christmas Day, my husband took my hand. "This is ridiculous," he said above the continued cries in the back seat. "I don't think it was realistic to think we could leave the house so quickly after this morning. We need to do something different."

I nodded, knowing exactly what he was talking about. We'd wanted to do what we'd always done, so we rushed our kids through Christmas morning at our house—wake-up, breakfast, gift opening, and getting ready to leave, with more family gifts and food yet to deliver. It turned out to be more than we could manage in one morning, and I felt terrible for not anticipating how taxing it would be for our young family.

As we drove along, I felt the stress of everyone in the car. When it was just Kyle and I, it had always worked out fine, going from one family gathering to the next. But now, with kids, it wasn't so easy. I was weary, and what we had done in the past no longer worked.

We needed time as a family to create some of our own traditions, and we needed more downtime and less stimulation. Although holiday celebrations are fun, they can also be tiring.

We needed rest.

Sitting quietly by the fireplace a few days after the merriment had ended and our overtired kids were sleeping soundly in their beds, we discussed what we wanted going forward.

"This isn't even enjoyable," I said. "I'm worried we're missing the most important aspects of Christmas because we're so busy running from place to place."

"I agree," Kyle responded. "We need to do something different."

"But what about our families? I don't want to disappoint anyone."

Kyle shrugged. "We need to do what's best for *our* family.

They'll understand. Or they won't," he said with a wink. "Either way, let's make a plan that we can both agree on."

I let out a sigh, knowing he was right.

Going into the next holiday season, we decided we would spend Christmas Eve with one side of the family and most of Christmas Day at home, visiting the other side of the family later in the day. We talked with our families weeks ahead of time about our new plan and why we needed to make a change. They graciously understood.

It was still a busy time, and our kids still got overstimulated with food, treats, and people, but overall, the days ran much more smoothly. As our kids have gotten older, we've changed some of our schedules again, adjusting for what works best for our family each year. But our goal is always the same: to connect with one another, with extended family, and with God, and to have fun while doing it.

We all will walk through seasons in life that will invite us to adjust—whether we're being swamped with work and a new career, accommodating school schedules, moving to a new place that's no longer close to family, or becoming empty nesters. The holidays are a time we need to be willing to adjust our schedules and expectations—and that's okay. It's a message I'm quick to share with others.

One dear friend called to say that she had just started a new job several states away from her family, and it was her first time to be away during the holidays. She was upset because some family members couldn't understand why she wasn't coming home to celebrate as she always had.

"But this is the job I've always wanted, and I can't take the time off," she said. "I feel bad. I want to be with them, but it's just not going to work this year."

"I understand," I said, explaining how we, too, had changed our family traditions over the years.

"What do you want to do?" I asked.

She thought about it. "I have time in January to return for a few days."

"Perfect," I said, and we talked about again letting her family know of the changes while also offering an alternative. In the end, some of her family decided to also come and visit her earlier in December to celebrate Christmas.

The world will always pressure us to be busier than we already are, and people's expectations will sometimes add to that pressure. But if we take the time to listen, Jesus will call us to rest in him. Even when life is chaotic. Sometimes, the best choice we can make is to say no to something that *may* be good so we can say yes to something that is *better*: Our sanity. Our peace. Our joy.

We don't have to be surprised by the changing seasons of life or feel bad when we need to make accommodations for our current life circumstances, nor should we begrudge others' need to do the same thing. Change is a part of life, and the Advent season isn't an exception. Some of us welcome change; for others, it can be challenging. But when our goal is to find ways to be present, enjoy the moment, and reflect on why we even celebrate in the first place, we'll not only accept change but embrace it.

And if we allow God to guide us through each stage of life, we can trust that he will do as he promised in today's verse, giving us water when we need it and restoring our strength for the tasks at hand. If we remain sensitive to his Spirit, we'll be like a well-watered garden or an ever-flowing spring, finding refreshment and rest for ourselves and also offering it to those around us.

*Lord, thank you for the different seasons of life. Thank you for what has been and for what is to come. Give us wisdom to know how to walk into this current season of life with grace and peace. Help us have honest conversations filled with love and compassion. Give us the courage to let go of things that no longer serve us and to allow others to adjust as they need to as well. We love you, Jesus. We are so grateful that you came. May we find the time to be with you and those we love. Amen.*

## Reflections:

1. Read Ecclesiastes 3:1-8. Spend some time thinking about your current season of life and how it meshes with your expectations for this Advent.

2. Traditions during the holidays are good, but sometimes they can hold us back from changes that need to happen. It's natural to be concerned about others' feelings, and we can certainly take them into account, but not at the expense of our own peace of mind. What conversations do you need to have with loved ones about expectations for the upcoming holidays and celebrations?

3. Now that you've spent some time considering your current season of life and how your traditions impact your relationships, what specific changes could you make to ensure peace and experience the joy of Advent?

## Embracing Advent:

*Make a plan for the holidays that will allow your family to engage in traditions while also carving out space for your current season of life.*

# The Joy of Presence

*You make known to me the path of life;*

*in your presence there is fullness of joy;*

*at your right hand are pleasures forevermore*

PSALM 16:11, ESV

MY UNCLE JIMMY WORKED at a paper mill, but his passion was horses. For decades, he and my aunt lived on a gravel road surrounded by dense trees, rolling hills, and farmland. Though he worked in town, he was most at home on the farm.

He always had quarter horses you could take for lazy rides down to Windy Lake and back, but his favorite breed was Belgians. The big draft horses were huge but beautiful. As a child, I (Kristin) had a healthy fear of their powerful bodies and their hooves, which I imagined were roughly the size of dinner plates. I'd often sidle along the edge of the stalls across from theirs, as far away from them as possible.

The one exception to my self-imposed rule was when Jimmy hitched them to the sleigh. He'd throw hay bales in the bed for seating, then he'd climb up to hold the reins and direct the horses with his booming voice. Bundled up against the biting cold, and with babies on their laps, the adults would sit and visit, swaying with the movement. The younger cousins sometimes used ropes to tie their plastic sleds to the back of the sleigh. As the horses trotted down the road, bells jingling, the kids would slide around behind, jockeying for position.

Corners were the most fun. Once, my dad decided to "ski" on his boots behind the sleigh alongside the kids on their sleds. He held on to a rope, sliding down the road just fine until we rounded a corner. Thrown off by the motion, he went flying into a snow-bank. We stopped, laughed, and waited for him to dust himself off and rejoin us.

Those memories are precious, not just because they remind me of how much I miss my uncle's boisterous laugh and the animated stories he'd tell, but because they perfectly encapsulated those days on the farm. No one was looking at a phone or distracted by a screen. Instead, we were fully immersed in the experience: the icy cold air in our noses, the wind on our faces, the slight hint of sweat under the many layers of winter clothes. Nothing could distract us from the joy of flying down that road at a brisk speed with loved ones around us and blinding white snow crunching under our sleds. Those memories are special because they helped me experience what I now recognize as the joy of presence.

Our need for one another is innate. Even the early church prioritized sharing meals and meeting together as a community. In fact, the author of Hebrews links gathering together with encouraging one another as a way to "motivate one another to acts of love and good works" (Hebrews 10:24-25). Spending time together positively influences us, but it also provides the motivation and connection we need as humans.

I love how today's verse, Psalm 16:11, talks about presence in terms of "fullness," as though it is a physical requirement like food or water: "You make known to me the path of life; in your presence there is fullness of joy; at your right hand are pleasures forevermore" (ESV). The author links our fullness—our overall satisfaction—with being in God's presence. Spending time in the Word or in prayer can help us encounter his presence. It's only through our relationship with him that we find true fulfillment.

But if the time spent in God's presence is when we are most connected to him, isn't the same true for our human relationships? After all, the presence of others helps us feel less alone and encourages us to face what lies ahead. It fills us with the warmth of contentment and reminds us that life is richer when lived alongside others.

On the other hand, a lack of face-to-face connections and true presence can spark a hunger for relationship that goes unsatisfied.

Despite the way technological advances make connecting with

others easier than ever before, many people feel incredibly lonely. Survey results vary, but 36 percent of respondents in one recent study reported feeling lonely "frequently" or "almost all the time or all the time" in the four weeks before the survey.[1] During the holidays, 55 percent of Americans report experiencing sadness and loneliness. The top reasons mentioned are being apart from loved ones (41 percent), having seasonal depression (37 percent), and coping with grief (36 percent), although over one-fourth of Gen Zers and millennials blamed social media for their loneliness.[2]

Those statistics represent millions of souls—friends, neighbors, family members, people in our community, or perhaps even ourselves—who feel disconnected from those around them. Maybe they are struggling with grief over a lost loved one or dealing with a difficult family relationship, and visions of other people's picture-perfect holidays amplify their own sadness. Whatever the cause, those feelings of disconnection can ultimately affect our physical well-being too. Over time, loneliness can increase our risk of heart problems, strokes, diabetes, depression, anxiety, addiction, suicidal thoughts or self-harm, and dementia. Any of these can shorten our life span.[3]

We aren't meant to live this life alone. That's why our presence—our real, unvarnished, authentic face-to-face connection—is so significant. When we think of the Christmas season, we often focus on what gift we're purchasing or which holiday events we need to attend. But the truth is that our undivided attention, one-on-one conversations, eye contact, and listening ear are often the greatest gifts we can give. Each of those gives others the gift of our presence.

In a distracted, distractible world, it can be hard to connect. One way is to begin being more intentional about setting aside our phones and laptops and spending time together in person. For instance, my friend Erin practices Sabbath with her family every weekend. She works at a church, so Sundays are a busy day. As a result, Friday evening to Saturday evening has become the twenty-four hours when they celebrate their Sabbath. She plans a Friday evening meal that her two young children will like. She lets them take turns choosing the dessert and bakes it with her young son when she's home during the day. Then, that night, she lights a candle for dinner, and the Sabbath begins. For the next twenty-four hours, she and her husband put their phones aside. They seek ways to feel restored as a family and as individuals. Together, they have fun as well as rest. This quiet rhythm has become a central part of their weekly routine.

Instead of getting pulled into the frantic round of Christmas events and obligations, let's enjoy our time together. Let's practice breathing deeply and savoring the moment we're in. Let's pause in our busy day to notice those around us: going out of our way to interact with cashiers at the checkout line, eating lunch in the break room with coworkers, checking in on a friend, or visiting with someone in the lobby at church. At home, let's sit quietly with the lights, music, and ones we love around us. When we ignore our screens in order to meet the eyes of those we see each day, we'll fill their hearts—and ours—with the gift of presence.

*Dear Jesus, thank you for your presence on this earth. Thank you for coming as an infant and for spending time with people face-to-face. Please give us the desire to focus on genuine, authentic connections with one another and the courage to make the changes we need for those connections to happen. Nudge us to set aside technology to pursue deeper relationships. Help us to notice those around us who are lonely. May we be reminded of the joy and contentment found in the gift of presence, both with you and with one another. Amen.*

## Reflections:

1. Read Hebrews 10:24-25. How does meeting together as believers motivate and encourage us? How have you seen this truth played out in your own life?

2. Think about friends or loved ones who may be feeling disconnected. How can you be intentionally present with them this week?

3. Reflect on the idea of finding "fullness," or overall satisfaction, in God's presence. How can you set aside time to focus on God and spend time in his presence fully?

## Embracing Advent:

*Decide on a length of time to put your phone aside today. Then, focus on giving the people you interact with your full attention.*

# Joe's Caramels

*My cousin Joe brought this recipe home from a home economics class more than forty years ago. Though he made it for many years, over time, my parents have made it their own annual tradition. I've spent many an hour placing cut-up caramels on wrappers, rolling them up, and securing the ends. It's the kind of recipe that's nice to make when you have a table full of helpers, ready to roll the caramels into individual portions. My mom says a candy thermometer is indispensable, as it's a delicate balance to ensure the caramels aren't too hard or sticky. These don't last long at our house but can be an excellent way to round out a plate full of cookies.*

## TOOLS

*Heavy 4-quart saucepan*
*8-by-11-inch buttered pan*
*Wooden cutting board*
*Candy wrappers for caramels (aluminum foil can also be used but is not as ideal as precut wrappers)*

## INGREDIENTS

2 cups sugar

1 cup butter; extra for buttering pan

1¾ cups light corn syrup

1 can (13 ounces) evaporated milk

4 teaspoons vanilla extract

1 cup finely chopped walnuts

## DIRECTIONS

1. In a heavy 4-quart saucepan, combine sugar, butter, corn syrup, and evaporated milk.
2. Cook over high heat, stirring frequently to 210 degrees Fahrenheit—about 5 minutes.
3. Reduce heat to medium. Continue cooking, stirring constantly, to firm ball stage (244 degrees Fahrenheit).
4. Remove from heat and immediately add vanilla and nuts, stirring quickly to blend.
5. Pour mix into buttered pan.
6. When thoroughly cold, loosen the candy from the pan and turn it onto a wooden cutting board.
7. Cut into small pieces (often rectangles, although they don't have to be) and wrap in candy wrappers.

*Makes 80 to 100 pieces.*

DECEMBER 21

# The 'Least' of Us

*That night there were shepherds staying in the fields nearby, guarding*
*their flocks of sheep. Suddenly, an angel of the Lord appeared among*
*them, and the radiance of the Lord's glory surrounded them. They*
*were terrified, but the angel reassured them. "Don't be afraid!" he said.*
*"I bring you good news that will bring great joy to all people.*

LUKE 2:8-10

"YOUR HANDWRITING IS BEAUTIFUL, JULIE."

Glancing at my paper name tag, I grinned. "Thanks! Unfortunately, this is as legible as it gets. I am a lefty."

And with that small confession, we found ourselves in an extended conversation about all things left-handed.

My colleague is originally from India, and it turns out that a generation or two back in that country (as well as in the United States), parents and teachers were forcing lefty children to become right-handed writers and eaters.

From my grandmother's stories, I knew about tying a child's left hand to force them to adapt to a right-handed lifestyle, a method used in parts of the United States, but I did not know that practice had been happening in India at the same time.

So, I asked the question: "Why?"

I had been told children were forced into right-handedness in the United States because of symbolism around evil, the devil, and being on the left side of God, although I have since learned that is only one of several reasons behind the practice. In India, at least one of the reasons had to do with notions of clean and unclean, the left hand being the unclean hand.

As my colleague and I considered the diverse cultural reasons for an identical practice, she smiled softly and said, "I guess our cultures share a tendency to suppress those who are different."

Her words hung between us for several heartbeats before the outside world intruded with the emcee returning to the podium. With a quick agreement to find time for a future coffee, we said our farewells and headed for our respective tables.

Since that fleeting conversation, I have thought a lot about human nature's tendency to demand conformity and create power dynamics. We create "in" and "out" groups within schools, work-places, churches, and beyond. We determine hierarchies of popularity based on notions of beauty, wealth, and power. And mostly, these ideas of conformity and power have nothing to do with godliness. In fact, many of our customs are in explicit violation of Scripture.

Jesus' earthly ministry is replete with stories and examples of turning our rules regarding conformity and power upside down and inside out.

On one such occasion, Jesus sought out a conversation with the chief tax collector in the region, Zacchaeus, pausing beneath the tree this man was perched in and inviting himself to stay at his house (see Luke 19:1-9). Tax collectors were notoriously corrupt and worked for the hated Roman authorities. Because Zacchaeus was the chief tax collector, he drew even more derision than his subordinates, yet it was his house in which Jesus asked to sleep.[1]

Another day, Jesus defended a woman caught in adultery, sparing her life as he wrote some unknown thing in the sand that caused her accusers—the religious leaders of the day—to drop their stones and go home (see John 8:1-11) even as he both forgave and redeemed her.

When asked to define who our neighbors are (and are not), in light of the commandment to love our neighbors as ourselves, Jesus told a story with a Samaritan (hated people group and enemies of the Israeli people) as the hero. This man stopped to help a robbery victim while a Jewish priest and a powerful community leader intentionally passed by, unwilling to assist (see Luke 10:27-37).

The exhortations in the Old and New Testaments to care for widows, orphans, foreigners, the poor, and the powerless leave no doubt as to God's view of our ungodly obsession with hierarchies and power (see Deuteronomy 10:18-19, for example).

But the two stories I love the most for showcasing just how little

God cares for our popularity contests and the chasing of human prestige are the stories that bookend the beginning and end of Jesus' time on earth: the announcements of his birth and his resurrection.

We'll come back to his birth announcement in a moment, but first let's consider the Resurrection. Many of us are well-acquainted with the general Easter story: Jesus was crucified on Friday, and on the third day (Sunday), he rose again, having defeated sin and death on our behalf. On the morning of his resurrection, he had a conversation with one person, Mary Magdalene, entrusting her to take the message back to the disciples that he was alive (see John 20:11-18).

In that culture and at that time, entrusting a woman to bear the message of his resurrection to the disciples and the world was the height of foolishness. Women were property, unable to testify in court, unable to bear witness, deemed utterly unreliable and untrustworthy to carry messages of any importance, let alone to tell the world that Jesus lived! Oh, how I cannot help but weep every time I read how Jesus valued and loved women and especially how he entrusted Mary to carry the good news of his resurrection back to the disciples and to the world!

The declaration of Jesus' birth, all those years earlier, was entrusted to a similarly disenfranchised people group: the shepherds.

Luke 2 tells us that a whole host of angels filled the night sky to announce the birth of our Savior with a spectacle worthy of such an occasion—to an audience of shepherds (see verses 8-14). Just as with women, shepherds at that cultural moment were bottom-of-the-hierarchy nobodies, humble peasants unable to testify or bear witness. Yet they were sent to meet the baby Jesus lying in a manger and to proclaim the angels' words to all who would listen.

If there was ever an invitation to give up our endless pursuit of popularity and to resist placing people into artificial, man-created categories that determine worth through beauty, position, wealth, and connection, it is embodied by the humble shepherd in your Nativity set.

I confess to dismissing the shepherds in Nativity sets I'd placed around my house for decades, casting the humbly dressed figures off to the side, sometimes even leaving them in the box entirely. Nowadays, a tiny shepherd sits all year long on my kitchen windowsill, an ever-present reminder that God loves all his children and that we have a scriptural command to do the same.

*Heavenly Father, forgive us for chasing after popularity and power. Forgive us for perpetuating "in" and "out" groups in our neighborhoods, schools, workplaces, extended families, and churches. Help us to see others as you see them: lend us your eyes, ears, and heart as we engage with those around us. Amen.*

## Reflections:

1. Read the full account of the angels appearing to the shepherds in Luke 2:8-20. How does the knowledge that shepherds were considered unreliable witnesses change your perspective of the story?

2. Read 1 Corinthians 1:28-29. What other verses or stories found in Scripture reveal God accomplishing his will through people who were usually disdained or deemed powerless?

3. In what ways have you allowed cultural notions of popularity and hierarchy to seep into your faith journey? In what ways has it colored your perspective of neighbors, members of your church community, coworkers, and parents next to you in the bleachers?

4. Prayerfully ask God to bring to mind people you've disdained or dismissed. Repent by seeking God's forgiveness, and if necessary, making a specific plan to interrupt the cycle.

## Embracing Advent:

*On a sticky note or index card, write a verse or a one-sentence summary of a biblical story as an instant visual reminder against the temptation to dismiss others based on cultural hierarchies.*

# Intentional Generosity

*All of us who have had that veil removed can see and reflect the glory*

*of the Lord. And the Lord—who is the Spirit—makes us more and*

*more like him as we are changed into his glorious image.*

2 CORINTHIANS 2:18

AS A CHILD, my dad was a Christmas Eve person. That is, he and his family opened gifts on Christmas Eve.

My mom, on the other hand, was a Christmas Day person. She and her family opened gifts on Christmas Day.

But when my parents married, my dad's parents—my mom's new in-laws—changed their tradition. Quietly and without fanfare, they became Christmas Day people. It wasn't until years later that my mom found out how they'd accommodated their habit to her own.

I (Kristin) love this story because it demonstrates how welcoming my grandparents were to my mom when she joined their family, and it is a beautiful example of generosity.

Christmas is a time of giving, but while we often focus on the many gifts we buy for loved ones and friends, it can be easier to overlook other forms of generosity displayed in the Christmas story.

Take the wise men, for instance. We don't know a lot about them, and in some ways, that makes their motivations and actions more intriguing. Why did they leave their home to search for an infant King? Did they think following the star would be worth the costs they incurred or the time they spent on the road? Why did they choose to bring the gifts they brought?

What we do know is that Matthew 2:1 refers to them as "wise men," although the term could also be read as "royal astrologers" or "magi." In *A Greek-English Lexicon of the New Testament*, the original Greek word *magoi* is defined as a "wise man and priest, who was expert in astrology, interpretation of dreams and various other occult arts."[1] While various sources wonder whether these visitors were kings, astrologers, or advisers to a distant ruler, we know that they visited from eastern lands, saw a star that they associated with "the newborn king of the Jews," and came to worship him (see Matthew 2:2).

Their first stop was the palace, where Herod met with them. Of course, it would seem logical that the king they sought would be in a palace, but he wasn't there. Did they wonder why he wasn't in such a likely place? Although they had studied prophecies, they may have had to revise their expectations.

After Herod told them where to find the infant and sent them on their way, the star they had seen guided them to Bethlehem and stopped over the place where Jesus was. The wise men responded with gladness: "When they saw the star, they were filled with joy! They entered the house and saw the child with his mother, Mary, and they bowed down and worshiped him. Then they opened their treasure chests and gave him gifts of gold, frankincense, and myrrh" (Matthew 2:10-11).

These gifts, of course, were the inspiration for our own gift giving. But the wise men weren't just generous in their gifts. They were also generous with their time. We aren't told how much time they committed to their trek, but it could have taken them a month or more to reach Bethlehem.[2] In addition, they were generous in setting aside their own desires. By leaving their homeland to seek Jesus, they became travelers on a journey that required them to forgo their comfort. As with my grandparents and their Christmas Eve to Christmas Day shift, generosity may mean we set our personal preferences aside for someone else's benefit.

Although we don't know which country they came from or how long it took them to arrive in Bethlehem, we do know that their actions required intentionality. They upended their lives to follow the star—and yet, isn't that what Jesus asks us to do too? Aren't we asked to upend our lives for him?

We don't often get asked to leave our homes behind, but our faith does require action and intention wrapped up in generosity—of our time, talent, or treasure—in service to others. And all of those things result in worshiping the King.

Generosity also requires discernment. When it was time to leave, the wise men avoided returning to Herod, who had falsely claimed he wanted to worship Jesus. In truth, Herod wanted to kill him. The wise men had been warned in a dream about Herod's intentions, but they still had to accept that the dream was an actual warning. They could easily have dismissed it or explained it away rather than recognizing its wisdom and truth. In the same way, we need to use discernment as we look for ways to be generous to others.

A generosity of spirit is more than giving of our time or money. It's not simply an action. Instead, it's who we are, an understanding that we are made in the image of God and reflect his likeness to the world. It's recognizing that God has been extravagantly generous to us by creating a beautiful world, giving us life, and meeting our needs. When we choose to be generous to others because it reflects God's model of generosity, it points others to him.

God's generosity toward us is extravagant, providing us with love, intention, time, compassion, and grace. How can we embody this kind of generosity? Maybe it's simply by assuming the best about other people's intentions or being willing to give them the benefit of the doubt when misunderstandings arise. Perhaps it's being more attentive to others so that we recognize what they need. Or it could require us to overlook small slights instead of escalating them, especially if the harm was unintentional. We reap what we sow, and when we sow generosity, we reap a harvest of kindness. Our actions follow our intentions, so if we begin by thinking generously, we'll be able to follow through with generous actions.

One year, my husband got a new grill. But after the delivery company dropped it off at our house, it sat on a pallet in the garage for months. Our friend Eli, who knew about its presence, stopped me one day on my way out of church.

"Hey, I know Tim will be gone for business this week," he said. "What do you think about Adam and me stopping over, putting the grill together for him, and moving it out of the garage?"

"Oh my goodness, he would love that!" I said, feeling relieved and grateful. They knew Tim had been too swamped with work to put it together and took time out of their schedules to help. Though their generosity was an action, it came about because they were attentive to the needs of others and noticed Tim's busy calendar.

In the same way, my friend Heather joked recently that her pantry was a graveyard of empty containers from meals people dropped off when she had a new baby. Although thrilled with the meals, she felt slightly overwhelmed at the prospect of returning all the containers. One friend had a unique solution. When she dropped off her meal, she told Heather, "Don't worry about the container. I'll drop off a coffee for you next week, and I can pick up the container then." What a thoughtful idea!

When we cultivate a generous spirit, we become more attuned to the needs of those around us. We are more willing to forgo our comfort or preferences in ways that are indeed acts of kindness for those who benefit. As we do, we'll grow more and more into the image of God, reflecting the likeness of his love into the world.

*Heavenly Father, thank you for your generosity. May our actions always reflect your generosity in ways that minister to and care for others. Give us wisdom and open our eyes to the needs of those around us so that we may cultivate a spirit of generosity. Amen.*

## Reflections:

1. Read Matthew 6:21 and 2 Corinthians 9:6. What do these verses reveal about how we should consider generosity?

2. What's an area where you find it easy to be generous? (Time, talent, treasure, etc.) What's an area in which generosity is difficult for you? In what ways could you embody the types of generosity God shows toward us— his love, intention, time, compassion, and grace?

3. Do you feel like you approach others with a generosity of spirit? Why or why not? How is generosity of spirit different from our typical definition of generosity? Based on the examples in today's reading, what could you do to develop generosity of spirit within yourself?

## Embracing Advent:

*Pray that God would give you the wisdom to see someone who needs generosity today. Then, follow through on providing it as well as you can.*

# Rejoice and Be Glad

*This is the day the LORD has made.*

*We will rejoice and be glad in it.*

PSALM 118:24

"WAIT, WHERE IS THE *FIRST PRESENT?*" I (Julie) called as I squished in next to my husband, Aaron. We'd just finished cleaning up after dinner, and opening presents was next on our agenda of Christmas Eve traditions with his family.

"I've got it!" my son, Jon, exclaimed, hoisting a medium-sized box above his head as he maneuvered from the Christmas tree to Aaron's side. "Here, Dad. I think this one is for you."

The twinkle in Jon's eye was unmistakable. As the current youngest in our extended family, he's given his dad this box every year for the last several. Each member of the next generation has taken their turn giving this particular gift over the years, each with their own flair for the dramatic.

"Oh. I have no idea what this could possibly be." Aaron's smirk as he bent to the task of unwrapping his gift matched the smirks around the living room. With the paper removed, Aaron popped off the tape, flipped the box flaps, and fished one arm around until he pulled out Louis the Cabbage Patch doll and held him aloft. We all cheered.

"Thanks, everyone. You shouldn't have," Aaron said with dry sarcasm. Chuckling, we shifted our attention to the actual presents waiting beneath the tree.

That's right, my husband gets a Cabbage Patch doll named Louis for Christmas. The same doll. Every year. For over thirty years. It's ridiculous and funny and one of my favorite Christmas traditions, despite occupying only a fleeting few seconds in our Christmas Eve celebration.

The story behind Louis involves a winning raffle ticket for the hottest toy of the year, an excited mom, a disappointed eight-year-old Aaron who didn't want a doll for Christmas, and then, years later, a practical joke on that same boy, now a teenager, that somehow turned into an annual event. It's the story of a Christmas flop redeemed into something silly and filled with loving affection for both Aaron and his mom. As much as I enjoy the goofiness of a practical joke that goes on into perpetuity, I'm in love with its redemptive arc and want to see it play out year after year.

And we're not the only ones with a quirky, fun tradition. My friend Carrie's family dines at Waffle House on Christmas. As with our tradition with Louis, they didn't set out to establish a new ritual, but kiddo taste buds and living too far from family finds them returning year after year. They pump Christmas tunes through the restaurant jukebox, laugh with staff and each other over ridiculous conversations, and leave an extra big tip as a thank-you and a blessing. Their joy carries them back out the door with full tummies and another good memory.

As lovely and fun as Carrie's and my traditions are, Christmas joy can be far simpler. In fact, sometimes joy is found in simplicity and ease precisely because it doesn't require energy or extra work. Every year, my friend Kate's family piles into their car with hot cocoa and Christmas cookies or candy canes and goes hunting for homes with light displays. It's a low-energy way for their entire family (with a wide age range of kids) to relax together as they ooh and aah over homes lit up with varying degrees of complexity. One house sets its light display to classic rock tunes, inviting families to park the car, tune in to a shortwave radio frequency, and listen to the Rolling Stones or the Beatles as the lights dance in time with the music. Driving around looking at Christmas lights has become a stress reliever for Kate and her husband, so they set out a couple of random evenings during Advent for an impromptu light tour when things start to feel tense around their home.

God has sent us every good gift (see James 1:17), and Advent is an invitation into an entire season of rejoicing. It's easy to dismiss the importance of funny moments and silly traditions in the face of the gravitas of God sending his beloved Son to us as an infant. After all, that tiny babe was predestined to a sacrificial crucifixion as the final blood offering to wash away forever our sin, thereby putting us back into right standing with God. While that gift is worthy of our somber reflection during Advent, it's also to be *celebrated* as we wring every ounce of joy out of December in a million tiny and big ways, some of which we've done for decades, and some of which are fleeting moments, unique to this day, this week, this year. Let us not forget that joy is listed as a fruit of the Spirit—tangible evidence that the Holy Spirit is active and at work in our lives (see Galatians 5:22-23).

Sacredness can be found in snowball fights and sledding and snow angels with your beloveds (or in going to the beach or into the desert for a picnic if you live in a land with a summery Christmas), in laughing so hard you can't catch your breath during the white elephant gift exchange or the ugly sweater contest, and in snuggling close while binge-watching Christmas movies. Worshiping God can look like pausing to deeply savor that first bite of perfectly cooked prime rib during your Christmas Eve dinner or sipping eggnog in the glow of your Christmas tree in those silent moments after everyone else is asleep.

Do not decline those invitations into joy and silly and fun sent your way this Advent. Look for them. Embrace them. Hold tightly to them. And then, invite others into merry and bright right along with you.

*Heavenly Father, thank you for invitations into joy this Advent as we celebrate and rejoice over the birth of your beloved son, Jesus. Help us seize those invitations and nudge us into inviting others to join in the fun. May this Advent be filled with laughter, with abiding contentment, and with a daily recognition of your goodness. Amen.*

# Reflections:

1. Read Galatians 5:22-23. How does knowing that joy is a fruit of the Holy Spirit change your perspective about the sacredness of fun, rejoicing, and delight? How does joy currently express itself in your life?

2. List events or activities that have brought you delight during Advent based on your five senses. In other words, what are the sights, sounds, tastes, textures, and scents that awaken your heart? These can be annual traditions or something new you'd like to try. How could you work more of them into your own Advent celebrations?

3. Ask two people to share something fun about their Advent season— a tradition, an activity, or something they savor. How do their answers spark new ideas for incorporating joy into your own celebrations?

# Embracing Advent:

*Make others laugh today. It could be a funny meme or video sent via text, a humorous card with a sweet note sent through the mail, a particularly groan-worthy dad joke told over the dinner table or at the start of a work meeting, a funny (mild) prank, or whatever else hits the particular funny bone of your loved ones.*

# The Thrill of Hope

*I pray that God, the source of hope, will fill you completely with*
*joy and peace because you trust in him. Then you will overflow*
*with confident hope through the power of the Holy Spirit.*

ROMANS 15:13

SCROLLING THROUGH A LIST of the most thrilling, dangerous things you can do on vacation, I (Kristin) can't say I've tried any of them. A cliff walk in China, ice swimming in Finland, skydiving near Mount Everest, free diving in the world's deepest known seawater blue hole in the Bahamas, a marathon in the Sahara Desert, and something called "volcano boarding" . . . Those all sound amazing—just not for me.

But I *have* strolled under the Eiffel Tower, gone white water rafting, glided through a glass-encased waterslide inside a shark-filled tank, climbed to the top of the Statue of Liberty, gazed at crystalline, turquoise glacial waters and lofty peaks from the heights of

Sulphur Mountain in Banff, ridden one of Europe's largest Ferris wheels (the London Eye), and breathlessly made it to the top of a fourteener in Colorado. Those experiences were unforgettable.

But the truth is, I don't think about them that often. Certainly not daily or even monthly. I'll recall them with fondness occasionally—especially if someone mentions them in conversation or asks about a certain location and it triggers a memory—but that's all. I don't dwell on them.

Unfortunately, the same can often be said about our response to Jesus. Stop to think about it: it is staggeringly impressive that the Savior of the world left behind the power and privilege of heaven to arrive on earth as a simple, helpless babe—knowing all the while that his purpose was to sacrifice himself to save us from our sins. If you and I are not constantly bowled over by how wild that feat was and by how it's changed the course of history, then we're due for a little reminder.

As an adult, fully human and with no hint of divinity within me, I find the idea of returning to infancy unfathomable. To transform from an autonomous being to a vulnerable child, as Jesus did, seems like an extreme proposition. Can you imagine willingly sending yourself into such a situation? I sure can't.

And yet, in a single act of matchless grace, that's what Jesus did. He came to earth, entrusting his care to fallible humanity. And the world has never been the same.

Jesus was the culmination of the world's collective hope. In him, all the Old Testament prophecies that people read about, dreamed about, and talked about for centuries were fulfilled. Isaiah 7:14, for example, spoke of how Jesus' birth would come about: "The Lord himself will give you the sign. Look! The virgin will conceive a child! She will give birth to a son and will call him Immanuel (which means 'God is with us')." The location of his birth, too—Bethlehem—was revealed long before Christ arrived (see Matthew 2:6, referencing Micah 5:2 and 2 Samuel 5:2).

Perhaps most familiar of all are the words of Isaiah 9:6, which speak to the hope that we have in Jesus:

> For a child is born to us,
>     a son is given to us.
> The government will rest on his shoulders.
>     And he will be called:
> Wonderful Counselor, Mighty God,
>     Everlasting Father, Prince of Peace.

The hope the world was clinging to and longing for was fulfilled in Jesus, our wise, powerful, and eternal Ruler, who brought reconciliation and peace between us and the Father. His birth was the spark that lit a global movement that has impacted millions, lasted thousands of years, and ministered to people from all over the world. That is astonishing!

And it's this same spark that lights a fire within *us*—if we'll only stop to consider these truths and allow them to kindle our awe of Jesus.

One of my favorite holiday traditions is the Christmas Eve service at church. Toward the end of the service, a single flame is lit by one of the pastors and then shared with everyone else in the audience. Candle by candle, the wavering flames move down the rows and across the aisles. They are held aloft by families, friends, acquaintances, and strangers alike. Music plays softly until the melody emerges and we begin to sing.

*O Holy night! The stars are brightly shining*
*It is the night of our dear Savior's birth*
*Long lay the world in sin and error pining*
*'Til He appeared and the soul felt its worth*
*A thrill of hope—the weary world rejoices,*
*For yonder breaks a new and glorious morn!*

As one, our voices strengthen to a triumphant crescendo.

*Fall on your knees; O hear the Angel voices!*
*O night divine, O night when Christ was born*
*O night, O holy night, O night divine!*

As I listen to the swell of singing all around me, emotion rises. Eyes full of unshed tears, I can't help but look down the row at my family and beyond them to friends and strangers, all coming together to celebrate the birth of a King. The beauty and mystery of a virgin birth, the stillness of the audience, and the miracle of the world's Creator coming to earth as Savior and King can all be felt in that hushed moment of collective wonder.

The promise and the hope of Jesus last long after the final note has been sung and the final flame has been extinguished. In Jesus, we receive the ultimate promise and the hope of eternity. Our soul feels its worth.

And just as the Old Testament prophecies were fulfilled when Christ arrived as an infant in Bethlehem, God still keeps his promises. Today's verse from Romans reminds us that God is the source of hope and that trusting in him helps us to "overflow with confident hope" because of the Holy Spirit within us.

This overflow of hope is what spills out of us—out of our overwhelming sense of awe—helping us to share the good news of Jesus. He is our hope, our light; he is our promise, forever.

*Dear Jesus, what hope we have in you! Thank you that your birth was the match that lit a flame of hope that can never be extinguished. May your light—the light of the world—always be our guide. Help us to feel fueled and renewed by the awe-inspiring events of your birth, life, death, resurrection, and ascension. Remind us that your promises are true and will remain forever. Let us continue to live a life full of hope as we place our trust in you. Amen.*

## Reflections:

1. What's a moment or experience from your lifetime that sparks feelings of awe or wonder? How often do you think about how memorable that moment was to you? If it's not that often, why not?

2. Read Psalm 86:8-10. What are some of the wondrous things God has done in your life? How has he kept or fulfilled his promises to you or your loved ones? How can reflecting on the promises he's kept in the past give us the courage to face each day anew?

3. Jesus' birth was a once-in-history event, but we've heard the Christmas story so many times that it can be easy to overlook its importance. How can you or your family recover the wonder of Jesus' birth by celebrating him today?

## Embracing Advent:

*Amid the noisy hubbub and celebrations of the next few days, find time to celebrate Jesus or simply to thank him for coming to earth and sharing his light with us.*

# Our Great Joy

*Suddenly, the angel was joined by a vast host of others—*
*the armies of heaven—praising God and saying,*
*"Glory to God in highest heaven, and peace on*
*earth to those with whom God is pleased."*

LUKE 2:13-14

AND SUDDENLY, the sky was filled with angels.

I (Kendra) imagine what that must have been like. But I'm not thinking about the shepherds looking up at that sight, although their story is important. I'm imagining what it must have been like for the angels.

They were present from the beginning of creation. They knew Jesus as God, and now they were seeing him come to earth, in human form, to save humanity and set right all that had gone wrong in the world.

"What love must God have for these people?"

"Do they know it?"

"What joy will they feel when they realize what his actions mean for them?"

I imagine they discussed these questions and more. And yet, they waited with anticipation for the appointed time.

How long did they know what God's ultimate plan would be? We're not told. But they knew it was on the horizon, and they would have seen it playing out before them.

They would have known of the angel appearing to Mary and then Joseph. They would have waited expectantly as Mary began to grow heavy with child. They would have observed as Elizabeth, moved by the Holy Spirit, called Mary blessed among women. They would have watched as Mary and Joseph traveled from their home in Nazareth to Bethlehem. For months, the excitement would have been brewing.

Until finally, one night in a stable in Bethlehem, Jesus arrived.

By that time, I'm sure they were more than ready to announce his birth as we read in Luke 2: "Suddenly, an angel of the Lord appeared among them, and the radiance of the Lord's glory surrounded them. They were terrified, but the angel reassured them. 'Don't be afraid!' he said" (verses 9-10).

What an experience for both shepherd and angel. Such a visit from the heavenly hosts has only happened (that we know of) a few times in history. Angels often work behind the scenes, but on this night, they were fully displayed for humans to see and hear. And I can almost feel their excitement.

The shepherds had almost certainly never seen an angel before. They must have looked at one another to ensure they were seeing the same thing. As the shock began to wear off, they surely would have wondered, *Why are they coming to us here?*

But before they could even ask, the angel brought an answer: "I bring you good news that will bring great joy to all people. The Savior—yes, the Messiah, the Lord—has been born today in Bethlehem, the city of David!" (Luke 2:10-11).

And then, as if the heavens couldn't hold back their excitement any longer, we read that "suddenly, the angel was joined by a vast host of others—the armies of heaven—praising God and saying, 'Glory to God in highest heaven, and peace on earth to those with whom God is pleased'" (Luke 2:13-14).

Other versions of Scripture use the word "multitude" to describe the number of angels. But what exactly is a multitude?

Hebrews 1:6-7 gives us a clue: "When he brought his supreme Son into the world, God said, 'Let all of God's angels worship him.' Regarding the angels, he says, 'He sends his angels like the winds, his servants like flames of fire.'"

This was no small event. *All* of the angels came to worship him. God didn't send just a few. He sent them all. Some believe the number of angels would have been as countless as the stars in the sky.

And I imagine they all *wanted* to be there to witness the most significant event of all time throughout all of history—and to finally be able to announce to the world that Jesus, the Savior, the Lord, the God of all creation, had arrived. What a moment of celebration for them. "He's here! Praise God! Glory to God!"

I can picture the celebration going on for quite some time on earth, just as it would have in heaven. The angels had been present at Creation, they were there for Jesus' birth, and they will be there at the end of the age when a new heaven and a new earth are ushered in. Glory to God.

Jesus arrives, and the angels are told to go and tell the shepherds. Not kings or queens. Not the wealthy or privileged. Just ordinary folks working their ordinary jobs. If the angels questioned the significance of bringing this news to shepherds, we see no sign of it.

They did as they were told. Having known God throughout the ages, they had to know his plan was good. They knew his motives were pure and just. His love for people was beyond comprehension. So they showed up, announcing the coming of the King who would usher in a new Kingdom—a Kingdom for those who, rather than seeking status or standing, would simply say yes to him. A Kingdom for those who would acknowledge him as Savior and entrust their lives to him as Lord.

What a glorious moment it must have been to witness as an angel.

And more than two thousand years later, we still celebrate that moment when heaven and earth came together in a very real way, to be witnessed by human beings. We still remember with awe that first Advent. But unlike many at the time of Jesus' birth, we now know the gravity of what Christ's coming to earth meant, just as the angels did on that day.

For that reason, we certainly celebrate his birth, but even more so his life, death, and resurrection, because of which we now have a blessed hope. He came to save us and to show us how to live here and now.

Do we take the time to truly celebrate his birth? To reflect and give thanks for his coming? To rejoice in the miracle of all that happened that first Advent?

I believe that if they could, the angels would come to us again today to remind us of Jesus' entry into the world as a babe. They would encourage us never to lose our awe over his arrival and never to stop announcing the coming of his Kingdom. Jesus' arrival was just the beginning of what was and is still to come. He is worth celebrating every day.

Let's proclaim on this Christmas Day, just as the angels did, Glory to God in the highest and peace on earth!

Yes, we know it now: his love, coming to us. His ways are shown to us, his life given so that we might live. So we celebrate, just as the angels did, what is now and has always been our great joy.

*Lord, thank you for the angels who announced your birth. How wonderful to think that both heaven and earth celebrated your arrival. Thank you for coming. May we never lose our awe over your arrival. We will forever celebrate your birth and what it meant for us and continues to mean, even now. We love you, Jesus. Thank you for loving us enough to come, to live among us, and to show us how to love. Amen.*

## Reflections:

1. Read Luke 2:8-20. Imagine being one of the angels that night. What thoughts or feelings would you have had as you announced the great news you had waited so long to share?

2. How would it have felt to have an angel announce to you the birth of Jesus? In what ways would it have changed your life afterward?

3. What was the significance of Jesus' birth, both for the shepherds and for us? Express your gratitude to God for the many blessings you enjoy because of this indescribable gift.

## Embracing Advent:

*After spending time in reflection, share with those around you the awe you have of Jesus' birth. Just as the angels did, tell someone what his arrival means to you.*

# Be a 'Light'

*The people who walk in darkness will see a great light.*
*For those who live in a land of deep darkness, a light will shine.*

ISAIAH 9:3

THE CELEBRATIONS HAVE ENDED.

The presents have all been opened. The tree and decorations will soon be put away.

I (Kendra) am always a little sad to see them go. Maybe it's because, living in the Midwest, I know that winter will soon envelop us fully, and sometimes it drags on a little too long. But it's also because I love the feeling of Advent. The twinkling lights. The warmth. The story of Jesus coming. The reminder of the hope we now have in him.

Jesus' birth is definitely worth celebrating, but it's not the end of the story. If we stopped there, we'd miss so much. We'd miss how he loved and cared for people, and how he called out those who thought they were being righteous but were really putting their rule-following ways above loving others. We'd miss his calling us to be his disciples and what it means to follow him. If we'd never observed his example in human form, we'd never wholly grasp that the greatest commandment is to love God and to love people, and that every other thing we do as followers of Jesus comes under that umbrella.

We'd miss his sacrifice, driven by his passionate love for us and for the world. We'd miss his desire to set everything right, to offer again a way for heaven to come to earth, and for us to experience it.

So now that Advent has ended, how do we take that same feeling, that same celebration, awe, and worship into the coming months?

We continue with the story. As we keep reading, we learn more about his purpose and his plan for us to be involved in it.

If you trust me, you are trusting not only me, but also God who sent me. For when you see me, you are seeing the one who sent me. I have come as a light to shine in this dark world, so that all who put their trust in me will no longer remain in the dark.

JOHN 12:44-46

He came to us who were living in darkness. He was the light we were waiting on. Until he came, we knew God, but only as a dim reflection of his true self. When Jesus arrived, he showed us perfectly who God the Father is and always has been. There is no longer a shrouding of his true character, love, mercy, and forgiveness. His justice. His welcome. Everything good and right and true about God is fully displayed in Jesus.

Now that Jesus has come and lived as our perfect picture of who God is, he calls us to be a light in the darkness too. And he tells us exactly how to do just that in John 13:34: "So now I am giving you a new commandment: Love each other. Just as I have loved you, you should love each other." We are now to go throughout our days loving others. It seems simple enough, but it can be challenging. Thankfully, we have help.

I will ask the Father, and he will give you another Advocate, who will never leave you. He is the Holy Spirit, who leads into all truth. The world cannot receive him, because it isn't looking for him and doesn't recognize him. But you know him, because he lives with you now and later will be in you. No, I will not abandon you as orphans—I will come to you.

JOHN 14:16-18

Once Jesus left the earth, he knew we'd still need help, so he sent an advocate, the Holy Spirit, to guide us each day. The Spirit doesn't abandon us but comes to us, reminding us of the light of Jesus that now shines through each of us.

When my husband Kyle and I had been married for only a few years, we attended a seminar that challenged us to love our neighbors. Our literal neighbors. The trainer had us draw a grid with our house in the middle and to list the names of the people who lived closest to us, as well as any details we knew about their lives— anything from where they worked to something hard they'd gone through in life.

Looking around the table as people filled their grids, I glanced at Kyle, feeling a little sheepish. We knew a few of our neighbors' names and one or two of their occupations but nothing personal about any of them. And we'd lived in our house for enough time that we really didn't have an excuse.

We went home, determined to get to know the people living closest to us. It wasn't easy, but we started with small conversations across the lawn, which led to yard parties, game nights, and birthday parties in garages.

What we found when we started inviting people into our lives was that they asked us right back. We've discovered deep friendships that have lasted years and even after we moved outside that neighborhood.

We recently celebrated our former neighbor Al's eighty-ninth birthday at KFC (his favorite restaurant). As we drove through our old neighborhood after lunch, he commented on how much he loved it when our kids would come over and visit. They'd bike around his driveway when the weather was nice, while he sat outside and watched.

If we had not reached out to him, we might never have known that Al is a widower without children of his own. Our relationship has grown over the years into a beautiful friendship that continues to this day. I couldn't have known where a simple smile and hello would lead. Today, it is our kids' pictures that hang on his wall, their drawings and cards that are stuck on his fridge. I'm grateful for the nudging of the Holy Spirit to reach out when we did; I'd hate to think of what we'd be missing out on today without Al.

We are all called to love those around us. For you, it may be in your school, your workplace, a volunteer opportunity, or your neighborhood. No matter who you are, if you are a follower of Jesus, the Holy Spirit will lead and guide you to people you can love well, people who may be lonely or in need of friends or even family.

We have no greater call beyond the Advent season than to love people well. That may look different for each of us, but the action of love is universally the same.

And when we love, we shine like lights, letting others feel and know the love of Jesus that we've experienced. That's the real reason we celebrate Christmas anyway.

His love—shown to us, so that we may show others.

*Lord, thank you for being the Light of the World. We're grateful that you came. May we experience and know just how much you love us. And then help us to have the courage to look around and love people well. We ask the Holy Spirit to nudge us this year when we can offer a bit of encouragement, compassion, and love to others. We're honored that you would use us as your hands and feet in this world. We love you. Thank you for loving us. Amen.*

## Reflections:

1. Now that the Advent season is over, what have you learned that you'd like to take with you into the new year?

2. Spend some time reflecting on what you've learned about God's character by observing Jesus' example. How could you better reflect his true nature to those around you?

3. Read John 14:2-28. How does knowing that Jesus did not leave us alone make you feel? How could you cultivate a greater awareness of the Holy Spirit's presence in your life? In what ways could you be more responsive to the Spirit in reaching out to others?

## Embracing Advent:

*Be intentional each morning about asking the Holy Spirit whom you can show God's love to that day, and determine to be a light of his love to others around you.*

# Bonus Advent Activities

## CHRISTMAS LIGHT SCAVENGER HUNT

Lights synchronized with music

Nativity scene

Angel

Santa Claus

Frosty the Snowman

Mrs. Claus

Rudolph the Red-Nosed
Reindeer

Presents

Star

Christmas wreath

Candy cane

Elf or elves

Sleigh

Inflatable snow globe

Train

Snowflake-shaped lights

Nutcracker

Window candles

Carolers

North Pole sign

Poinsettia

Giant ornaments

Stocking

Gingerbread house or man

"Joy" sign

## HOW TO INCORPORATE KIND ACTS
## INTO THE ADVENT SEASON

1. Compile a list of things you are passionate about—such as foster kids, taking care of animals, homelessness, or food insecurity— and then find an organization that addresses that issue and volunteer.

2. As you make your list, think about things you can do in your neighborhood, community, state, country, and the world.

3. Come up with little ways to show kindness throughout your days—say hello, hold the door for others, invite a new person to lunch or to sit by you.

4. Plan ahead: choose your kind acts at the beginning of December, then plan specific days or times to accomplish them.

5. During breakfast or supper, reflect on what you plan to do or have done that day, and if doing it with your family, discuss it together.

## 10 SIMPLE TRADITION IDEAS

1. Find an Advent wreath you love and use it throughout the Advent season. You can light the candles as your dinner table centerpiece or light them later and set the mood for an evening conversation in which each person shares three things they are grateful for that day.

2. Make a seasonal recipe you save for this time of year.

3. Read the Christmas story together as a family on Christmas Eve or Christmas Day.

4. Watch Christmas movies with friends or family. Pick a favorite one to watch year after year and try a new one each year. (Our family favorites include *The Nativity Story*, *Elf*, and *Frosty's Winter Wonderland*.)

5. Attend a Christmas play, concert, or choir performance. (Many community or church choir concerts and other performances are free or low-cost.)

6. Send a warm note of thanks (a child's artwork inside a card is always a special touch) to a different group within your community each year: first responders, the public works department, ER staff, teachers, school lunchroom personnel, your pastor, or anyone else whose service is often overlooked.

7. Attend a candle lighting service on Christmas Eve or a sunrise service on Christmas morning.

8. Spend fifteen silent minutes in the glow of the Christmas tree with a favorite warm beverage before the day begins or after everyone else is in bed.

9. Make decorating the tree a festive family event with fun snacks, lively Christmas music, and grace for weirdly placed ornaments! (This makes an especially beloved tradition for Grandma and Grandpa's tree if they live nearby.)

10. Create a Christmas music playlist to listen to every time you are in the car or for other festive moments. Don't forget to crank the volume and make everyone sing along—no matter how badly you sing!

## 5 WAYS TO CELEBRATE JESUS' BIRTH

1. Bake a cake, light candles, and sing "Happy Birthday" to Jesus.

2. Make birthday cards or ornaments for the tree to celebrate Jesus.

3. Have everyone share one reason they are grateful that Jesus came.

4. Sing Christmas carols together.

5. Find a Christmas movie that celebrates the birth of Jesus, and watch it as a family.

# Notes

INTRODUCTION
1. Heidi Godman, "How to Make the Holidays Less Stressful," *U.S. News and World Report*, March 27, 2023, https://health.usnews.com/wellness/articles/how-to-relieve -holiday-stress.

WHAT'S MOST IMPORTANT
1. Our experiences ultimately led to a whole book, in case you'd like some other ideas: *The One Year Daily Acts of Kindness Devotional: 365 Inspiring Ideas to Reveal, Give, and Find God's Love* (Carol Stream, IL: Tyndale House Publishers, 2017).

REFRAMING OUR EXPECTATIONS
1. Albert Barnes, "Commentary on Matthew 1," *Barnes' Notes on the Whole Bible*, https://www.studylight.org/commentaries/eng/bnb/matthew-1.html.
2. E. H. Plumptre, "Matthew 1," in *Ellicott's Commentary for English Readers*, ed. Charles John Ellicott, https://biblehub.com/commentaries/ellicott/matthew/1.htm.

GOOD GIFTS
1. American Psychiatric Association, *Holiday Stress*, November 2021, https://www.psychiatry .org/File percent20Library/Unassigned/APA_Holiday-Stress_PPT-REPORT_November -2021_update.pdf.

THE OVERLOOKED MAIN CHARACTER
1. Larry Dossey, "The Helper's High," *EXPLORE* 14, no. 6 (November 2018): 393–399, https://doi.org/10.1016/j.explore.2018.10.003.

### RECOGNIZING JESUS

1. Soo Kim, "How Finding 'Glimmers' of Hope in Day to Day Life Improves Mental Health," *Newsweek*, July 23, 2023, https://www.newsweek.com/mental-health-crisis -glimmers-trauma-therapy-viral-tiktok-1814542.

### THE JOY OF PRESENCE

1. Richard Weissbourd et al., *Loneliness in America: How the Pandemic Has Deepened an Epidemic of Loneliness and What We Can Do about It*, (Cambridge, MA: Making Caring Common Project, Harvard Graduate School of Education, February 2021), https://mcc.gse.harvard.edu/reports/loneliness-in-america.
2. Michelle Lambright Black, "55% of Americans Struggling with Holiday Loneliness, While Many Aren't Fully Satisfied with Their Mental Health Insurance Coverage," ValuePenguin, January 3, 2022, https://www.valuepenguin.com/holiday-loneliness -survey.
3. "Health Risks of Social Isolation and Loneliness," Centers for Disease Control and Prevention, March 30, 2023, https://www.cdc.gov/emotional-wellbeing/social -connectedness/loneliness.htm.

### THE LEAST OF US

1. "Luke 19:2" study note, *NLT Illustrated Study Bible* (Carol Stream, IL: Tyndale House, 2015).

### INTENTIONAL GENEROSITY

1. Frederick William Danker, ed., *A Greek-English Lexicon of the New Testament and Other Early Christian Literature*, 3rd ed. (Chicago: The University of Chicago Press, 2000), 608.
2. Mark Ward, "What Do We Really Know about the Three Wise Men?" Logos, December 7, 2017, https://www.logos.com/grow/really-know-three-wise-men/.

# About the Authors

JULIE FISK left a fifteen-year legal career to become an author. Always passionate about words, she shifted her storytelling from courtrooms and boardrooms to telling stories of God's faithfulness, no matter the circumstance. Julie is a national speaker and coauthor of several books. Together with her cofounders of The Ruth Experience, Julie connects with an online community of women seeking and living out their faith. When she's not writing or speaking, Julie is a backyard farmer, a collector of coffee mugs, and an admitted bookworm.

Do it afraid. KENDRA ROEHL has sought to live out that advice as a social worker, foster parent, mother of five, and public speaker. She has a master's degree in social work and has naturally become a defender of those in need, serving others in hospice, low-income housing, and veterans' affairs programs. Kendra and her husband are well-known advocates for foster care, taking in more than twenty children in six years and adopting three of them. As a cofounder of The Ruth Experience, she continues to care for others as a frequent speaker and an author of several books.

A career in journalism set KRISTIN DEMERY up to one day publish her own stories of living this wild, precious life. She is now an author of several books and part of a t`rio of writers collectively known as The Ruth Experience. Kristin served as a newspaper and magazine editor, and her work has been featured in a variety of publications, including *USA Today*. She still works behind the scenes as an editor for others while writing her own series on kindness, friendship, and living with intention. An adventurer at heart, she loves checking items off the family bucket list with her husband and three daughters.

# Journaling Pages

# Also from
# Tyndale House Publishers

*Available at Tyndale.com or wherever books are sold!*

CP1970

Glory to God in highest heaven,
and peace on earth to those with
whom God is pleased.

**LUKE 2:14**